"*How Is Greater Than What* is a genuinely engaging journey of personal enlightenment. In a refreshingly candid and self-disclosing style, Preston Poore takes you inside his daily work life, revealing missteps, successes, and lessons learned. He has poured his soul into this book, and his central message comes across on every page: *how* you travel through work and life is the most significant guiding principle. Filled with relatable true stories and practical tips, Preston's journey reveals how devoting oneself to personal growth and caring for others can liberate the leader in everyone. I encourage you to see for yourself how he came to this realization and how you can benefit from his experience."

    – JIM KOUZES, coauthor of the bestselling *The Leadership Challenge*

"In How is Greater than What, Preston Poore offers a powerful reminder that true leadership is not just about achieving results—but about how we achieve them… This book is a must-read for anyone who wants to lead with both excellence and purpose. Let Preston's insights inspire your own transformational journey as a leader."

    — DEE ANN TURNER, Former Vice President, Chick-fil-A, Inc. Best-selling Author of *Bet on Talent and Crush Your Career*

"How Is Greater Than What is a fantastic resource for today's leader… a leader who understands that HOW they approach leading is oftentimes more important than WHAT they are delivering. Today's leader must have a dual focus on leadership while continually developing their leadership skills and this book is a wonderful accelerator to this development journey."

    — ERIC BLUMENTHAL, Sr. Vice President, Foodservice Division, The Coca-Cola Company

"Honest, practical, and rooted in wisdom earned from the front lines of leadership. This is more than a book—it's a guide to significance."

— **GARRY RIDGE**, Bestselling author of *Any Dumb Ass Can Do It*, Chairman Emeritus, WD-40 Company & The Culture Coach

"Drawing from his rich corporate and nonprofit experience, Preston Poore offers transformative insights and exercises that empower leaders to grow personally and professionally, leading with greater integrity, authenticity, and impact."

— **JORDAN RAYNOR**, bestselling author of *Redeeming Your Time*

"Leaders are always pursuing more influence. That's not a bad thing. But are we approaching our goals the right way? Preston's experience, heart, and message will help you put first things first in how you lead."

— **TAMI HEIM**, President & CEO, Christian Leadership Alliance

"*How Is Greater Than What* is a necessary gut punch. Preston Poore doesn't write from theory; he writes from scars. This isn't a book about climbing ladders; it's about walking worthy. It's about leading in a way that does more than just impress people. The stories are raw. The insights are earned. And the message is clear: your methods matter. In a culture that celebrates outcomes and overlooks character, this book calls leaders back to the narrow road where integrity, humility, and Christlike influence shape what truly lasts. I didn't just read this; I sat with it. Highlighter in one hand, mirror in the other. If you lead people, I recommend you do the same."

— **CHRISTOPHER SIMPSON**, President & CEO, CBMC International

"*How Is Greater Than What* is not only a great book, but a foundational truth that positively impacts the way we work *and* the way we relate with everyone in our lives. There is an abundance of excellent guidance in this book to help us become better leaders, and it's woven with so many stories and examples that enable us to connect and relate—the good, the bad, and the reality that we are all imperfect and growing. Process, People, and Purpose are at the center of everything, and that is powerful!"
— **JULIE NEE**, Vice President, The Jon Gordon Companies & former Hershey Companies executive

"Through vivid storytelling, actionable takeaways, and a cohesive narrative, Preston Poore has perfectly captured the essence of inspired leadership. His genuineness and authenticity come through on every page. *How is Greater Than What* is destined to be essential reading for both budding and seasoned leaders."
— **PETER J. DE SILVA**, L.H.D, Best Selling Author & CEO IRALOGIX

"Truly great leaders are more focused on the journey than the destination. In the long run, how we do things along the way is more important than where we end up. People care and they notice. Ultimately, a leader's legacy will be defined by their "How". Preston does a great job of driving this journey attitude home in his new book, *How Is Greater Than What*.»
— **TODD HOPKINS**, International Best-Selling Author and Founder of Office Pride & Strategic Thinking Network

"As CEO of the Charcot-Marie-Tooth Research Foundation, I enthusiastically endorse this impactful book that redefines leadership by emphasizing how we lead is far more important than the outcomes we achieve. In a world often focused on immediate results, this book reminds us of the essential qualities of purposeful, empathetic leadership. Its insights are applicable across various fields, including healthcare and research, and encourage readers to reflect on their journeys while embracing values that foster trust and collaboration. For anyone seeking to make a meaningful impact, this book provides a roadmap for positive change and inspires the cultivation of a transformative leadership legacy."

— **LAURA MACNEILL**, CEO, CMT Research Foundation

"If you're looking for and a great way to make this world and your work better, you've picked upthe right book. Preston's authentic stories and breadth of leadership experience will guide you to a life of significance and deeper purpose."

— **KENT CHEVALIER**, Athletes in Action, Pittsburgh Steelers Chaplain

"A must-read for values-driven leaders. In *How is Greater Than What*, Preston reminds us that success isn't just about the destination. It's about how we choose to get there. With clarity and conviction, he shows us that integrity, ethics, and moral discernment are not just ideals, but essential tools for the impact that lasts beyond the destination."

— **DEAN CROWE**, Founder & CEO, Rally Foundation

"Preston Poore's book is a rare combination of profound and entertaining. It starts at full speed with a story that sucks you in, and it kept me hooked the whole time. I highly recommend this book for anyone looking for a life of meaning and success. It turns out that the noble path is also the most productive path in the end, too."

— **SCOTT WOZNIAK**, Author of *Make Your Brand Legendary* and CEO of Swoz Consulting

"Preston's book is a must-read for leaders who want to elevate their performance and become better human beings in the process. With a blend of real-life storytelling and practical advice, he addresses the challenges faced by today's leaders—whether feeling burned out, disconnected, or struggling to build trust. This book offers invaluable insights for anyone seeking to lead with impact, purpose, and integrity in a rapidly changing world."
— **ELIZABETH DIXON**, President, CEO, Trilith Foundation & Founder, CEO Slumber Sleepware

"How many times will a leader drive through the pothole of *'It's not what you said, it's how you said it'* before making the single greatest change necessary to catalyze people, fortify culture and drive outcomes? In *How Is Greater Than What,* Preston Poore skillfully guides leaders to remove the primary obstacle to their success…inattention to the humanity of leadership …and replace it with the authenticity, purpose and meaning necessary to achieve greatness."
— **SCOTT CALDWELL**, President, CLC (Christ Led Communities)

"Preston Poore's *How>What* is a powerful guide for emerging leaders who aspire to make a meaningful impact in their organizations. Preston brilliantly connects the dots between purpose, leadership, and personal growth, emphasizing that how we lead is far more important than just what we achieve. His insights resonate deeply with my belief that leadership begins with personal transformation. This book is a must-read for anyone looking to elevate their leadership game and make a lasting difference."
— **CLAY SCROGGINS**, Author of *How to Lead When You're Not in Charge*

"As an officer in the US Air Force, I learned if leaders take care of their people, their people will take care of the mission. In *How Is Greater Than What,* Preston Poore makes a compelling case for why your organization's people and the process matter more than its end product."

— **DARREN SHEARER**, Author, *The Christ-Centered Company*

"How Is Greater Than What not only redefines what success looks like but also lights the path for those striving to leave a positive mark on the world, by living a life of significance. You will walk away not just inspired, but equipped—ready to lead, to serve, and to build your legacy defined not by titles or accolades, but by the lives that you have touched along the way."

— **MARK WHITACRE**, Vice President, Culture & Care & Executive Director of t-factor, Coca-Cola Consolidated, Inc.

"Most leadership books focus on one of three areas: vision, strategy, or results; all vital aspects of building a successful organization. However, in *How Is Greater Than What,* Preston Poore makes the compelling case that the true differentiator in leadership, the thing that is catalytic in everything you do as a leader, is your *how*. How you communicate, How you execute. How you develop people. And how you develop yourself. Whether you lead a large corporation or a start-up non-profit, *How is Greater Than What* will help you build the imperative foundation to help you become a successful leader people will want to follow."

— **KEVIN MARKS**, Passion Publishing and Conferences

"Preston Poore has delivered another book that pulls from his extensive corporate experience and fuses that with insights from his life and personal network to produce a must read for today's leaders as well as the leaders of tomorrow."

— **DR. CHARLES M (CHAD) CARSON**, Ph.D., Professor of Management, Brock School of Business, Samford University

"As someone who has lived at the intersection of faith and the corporate world, I found *How is Greater Than What* to be both deeply relatable and profoundly convicting. Preston's honesty, practical wisdom, and Christ-centered values offer a much-needed paradigm for leaders who want to do more than climb ladders—they want to elevate people."

— **STEVE ADAMS**, Co-founder and Executive Director, Embracing Brokenness Ministries

"I've found that if you get the top button of a shirt wrong, all the others are off; but if you get that one right, all the others line up. Through his journey and learnings, Preston Poore brilliantly tells us how to get the top button of work, life, and faith right and see alignment and significance flourish. This is leadership that works!"

— **DR. MICHAEL SPRAGUE**, Louisiana State Chaplain, Capitol Commission

"Preston's insights perfectly resonate with my leadership journey, offering clarity on how our approach to challenges speaks louder than the tasks themselves. The book brilliantly captures this idea but goes even further by offering practical steps elevate leadership."

— **EDWIN GOTAY**, Managing Director, Partnership Marketing, NASCAR

"Most first time managers step into that role blissfully unaware of what's really required to effectively lead. We know what needs to happen, but when it comes to the how - well; that's just death by a thousand paper cuts. In *How Is Greater Than What*, Preston Poore articulates clear, simple and practical action steps to make that jump. I wholeheartedly recommend this to any leader, regardless of what stage they're at in their career."
— **MATT TRESIDDER**, CEO, Co-Founder, Leadr

"Preston Poore's *How Is Greater Than What* beautifully captures something I've come to believe with my whole heart: the way we treat people along the way matters just as much as what we accomplish. In a world chasing metrics and milestones, this book is a call back to the deeper work—building trust, honoring others, and creating a culture where people and performance thrive together. It's a refreshing reminder that how we lead is what ultimately defines the legacy we leave."
— **JOSH BLOCK**, President of Block Imaging and Founder of People Matter at Work

"*How Is Greater Than What* is a must-read for anyone who wants to take their leadership to the next level. Preston Poore shows us that it's not about the destination, but how you get there. You want inspiration? It's here. You want hilarious stories? It's on the next page! You want a book to give to your friends? (whispers) You're holding it. Thank you, Preston, for writing this book!
— **ROSS KIMBALL**, Actor (Jury Duty, other things), Comedian, Speaker, Founder of Show Up Better Communications

"There is no shortage of people who are quick to tell you what to do but finding people who will take the time to show you how, that is a treasure. This is how true leaders lead, and how real impact is made. Preston's book How is Greater than What, is the bold call to action that leaders need to make the true impact that they were created for and called to."

    — **DAVIN SALVANGO**, bestselling author of Thieves of Purpose, Co-founder of The Purpose Summit

"In a business landscape obsessed with outcomes, "How is Greater than What" brilliantly shifts our focus to the transformative power of process. The culture one builds as a leader, the sustainability of results over time are inextricably link to they kind of people we are. "How you show up as a leader ultimately determines lasting success. This practical read provides executives with a comprehensive framework for building influence brick by brick, navigating disruption with resilience, and creating elite client experiences that set you apart in any market. Whether you're leading a startup or steering an established enterprise, this book will fundamentally change how you measure success and build a legacy that transcends mere results."

    — **DR. CHIP ROPER**, CSO/Managing Partner of RKE Partners, President VOCA Center, Board Chair of the New Canaan Society

"*How is Greater Than What* provides proven principles and guidelines on leadership and innovative ways of growing influence with sincere, selfless motives. It emphasizes the value of knowing your purpose and calling and the importance of being authentic in leading and serving others. This book is a must-read for up-and-coming public safety leaders."

    — **DR. KELVIN J. COCHRAN**, Former U.S. Fire Administrator; Former Fire Chief of the City of Atlanta, GA, and the City of Shreveport, LA

"Preston has poured himself into this book by sharing personal, vulnerable and helpful stories of why it is so important to know the 'how' rather than the 'what' to accomplish great things as a leader. As a seasoned business executive with the largest corporations, he uses his teaching, coaching and communication skills to document in this book what thousands have already heard in his training sessions. Preston is now willing to share this in his crafted handbook for knowing the reason behind effective leadership. I've always felt there was a difference between being a boss, a leader, or an owner. Preston articulates that difference so well and encourages those who aspire to nurture, protect and provide are those who are easily followed. Preston's uses incredible word pictures, quotes, and stories to communicate. He followed the example of how Jesus communicated so well and is successful with this great work. I highly recommend this to all who aspire to become effective and truly successful in this world and the next."

– **RAYMOND H HARRIS,** Architect, author, executive movie producer, venture capitalist in God's kingdom

"Regarding Preston's *How is Greater Than What,* I just want to say, YES! YES! YES! YES! Everyone (and I'm not over-stating that) needs to read, embrace and apply the clearly and compellingly communicated principles and practices he lays out in its easy-to-read pages. It will prove revolutionary for your personal life and whatever influence you are able to bring to any team and/or organization you have influence in or over. Preston has brilliantly captured and articulated what we at MHCC have intentionally pursued over the years in our quest to build a transformative culture. Read it, enjoy it, and be changed by it."

> **– TOM GRAY**, Senior Pastor, Mars Hill Community Church, Powder Springs, GA & President, This Stuff Matters

"Though we might first look at the leaves and branches, the ultimate health of a tree is fundamentally determined by its roots. I loved delving into *How is Greater than What* because Preston Poore skillfully unpacks a reality too often overlooked in leadership philosophy and coaching: the primary importance of the 'root system' in our leadership — roots like identity, purpose, character, courage, and integrity. Through keen observation, practical wisdom, and personal experiences, he invites us into beneath-the-surface habits which foster healthy, impactful influence while guiding us away from the danger of being so fixated on the 'what' in our leadership endeavors that we neglect the all-important 'how.'"

> **– MATT HEARD**, President of Thrive Fully Alive, Inc. and author of *Life with a Capital L: Embracing Your God-given Humanity*

"*How Is Greater Than What* is a groundbreaking guide that redefines the path to success. The book's central thesis asserts that focusing on the "how"—the actionable steps and strategies—is more critical than dwelling on the "what." Through a combination of compelling stories and probing questions, author Preston equips leaders with the tools to ask the right questions and foster meaningful change. This book is an essential read for anyone seeking to accelerate their personal and professional development."
  — **BILL FORSTER**, CEO of CEO Zones

"Many leadership books, even those written by Christian leaders, often focus on metrics and measurables. Those are important, but Preston Poore presents something most neglect: the interior life of the leader. This book is both practical and deep and will challenge leaders from the smallest startups to Fortune 500 companies, from church planters to megachurches."
  — **DANIEL DARLING**, Director of The Land Center for Cultural Engagement at Southwestern Seminary and author of *Agents of Grace, A Way with Words,* and *The Dignity Revolution*

"We've all had a bad day at work. In fact, Preston shares one of his at the beginning of the book. But what we do next can make all the difference. A turn-around can happen. It's all in the How."
  — **JEFF HENDERSON,** author of *Know what you're FOR. A great strategy for work, an even better strategy for life*

HOW IS GRE>TER THAN WHAT

Master the Growth and Leadership Skill Everyone Else Ignores

PRESTON POORE

HOW IS GREATER THAN WHAT
Master the Growth and Leadership Skill Everyone Else Ignores

Preston Poore

© Preston Poore. All rights reserved. No part of this publication may be reproduced, distributed, or transmitted in any form or by any means, including photocopying, recording, or other electronic or mechanical methods, without the prior written permission of the Exactly Press, except in the case of brief quotations embodied in critical reviews and certain other noncommercial uses permitted by copyright law. For permission requests, please contact the author.

Scripture quotations used by permission. All rights reserved.

The Message, copyright © 1993, 2002, 2018 by Eugene H. Peterson. of NavPress. Represented by Tyndale House Publishers, Inc.

The ESV® Bible (The Holy Bible, English Standard Version®). Copyright © 2001 by Crossway, a publishing ministry of Good News Publishers.

Back cover photo: Bonnie Heath

ISBN: 979-8-218-76065-6

Printed in the United States of America.

PrestonPoore.com

To Caroline and Benton.
My favorite children and my greatest joy.

This book is packed with lessons, some hard-earned.
My hope? That these pages help you lead with
purpose, live with integrity, and love without regret.

This is for your generation—and the one coming next.

Contents

Introduction: How Sunset Cinema Shaped a Leadership Philosophy 19

Chapter 1: Start with Who? 29

Chapter 2: Driving with Purpose. 45

Chapter 3: The Mission of Vision 63

Chapter 4: Talk Is Cheap 83

Chapter 5: Stop Building Trust. 101

Chapter 6: Titles Don't Matter. 121

Chapter 7: Dancing with Wolves. 143

Chapter 8: Do You Believe?. 159

Chapter 9: Cutting Through the Noise 179

Chapter 10: Plans Don't Win 195

Chapter 11: Change or Be Changed 217

Chapter 12: What's That Smell?. 235

Epilogue: True Identity 259

How Is Greater Than What Principles. 268

Acknowledgements. 269

The Free Workbook That Turns Insight into Action. 273

Formed to Lead 275

Make Better Decisions One Day at a Time .277

Transform Your Team. Learn the *How*. 278

Coaching and Consulting. 279

Notes and References 281

INTRODUCTION

How Sunset Cinema Shaped a Leadership Philosophy

"If at first you don't succeed,
then skydiving definitely isn't for you."
– STEVEN WRIGHT

It was a typical hot evening in the deep South—the kind of night when sweat won't stop drenching your clothes. Sometimes, the only relief is an ice-cold Coca-Cola to quench the thirst and cool down your forehead.

When the movie ended, the tiny crowd began climbing up the outdoor amphitheater steps toward the exit. They'd come to our first "Sunset Cinema" event with the promise of entertainment and refreshment. What should have been a success fell flat.

I was visibly agitated and jumped into a heated conversation with my key stakeholder. He was even more disappointed, and, frustratingly, he was right.

"It's not what you did, Preston," he shot back. "It's how you did it."

Those words still echo in my ears.

I was new to the Coca-Cola System's hyper-competitive and politically charged environment, which included The Coca-Cola Company (TCCC), bottling partners, customers, and consumers.

Nine months earlier, they had hired me as a "franchise leader" to strategically align with their largest bottler and local leadership team to inspire flawless execution of marketing initiatives. Ultimately, my job was to influence the Coke System and achieve revenue, profit, and market share goals in the area. Expectations were high.

Interestingly, I didn't have direct reports but multiple internal and external stakeholders (e.g., operations, manufacturing, media, marketing, sales, marketing assets, former owners, legislators, etc.). There were a lot of cooks in the kitchen, but I viewed that as a positive. *It shouldn't be too hard,* I told myself. *I'm known for getting things done regardless of the collateral damage.*

But when I arrived in Montgomery, Alabama, I discovered that the territory's performance had no fizz. Over two years, the bottler drove the marketplace into the ground. Sales were down, the customers weren't happy, and consumers were losing that loving feeling. Even worse, employee morale tanked because of recent difficulties with the management transition. The new leadership experienced high employee turnover, including merchandisers, drivers, and managers, and execution challenges like out-of-date products, empty shelves, and coolers.

The primary competitors, Pepsi and their local bottler, Buffalo Rock, were nipping at our heels—so much so that our market share shrank from an amazing 70% to below 50%. If you're familiar with the world of consumer products, market share is a lagging indicator of how healthy brands and products are and how they stack up against the competition. Fifty percent may sound great to a normal market, but Montgomery and the surrounding area were an exceptionally high share market in the past. It was a turnaround job, for sure.

Despite the challenge, I was already thinking beyond this role. I believed that if I could make it in Montgomery, I could make it anywhere. (Not exactly New York, but you get the point.) I had six successful years at The Hershey Company in sales and commercial roles, was a top performer and individual contributor, and won two President's Cups – national sales performance awards. Was I cocky? Yes. Maybe even arrogant, some might say. Well, a lot would say.

I saw Montgomery as a means to my ambitious ends. Do well there, impress the Market Unit Vice President, and get promoted to Atlanta, the Coca-Cola Mecca. Then, I'd climb the corporate ladder and finally prove myself to everyone. Just wind me up and let me go. Promotions, recognition, money, and prestige waited for me on the other side of this gig. All I needed to do was start well in Montgomery, and my career would take flight.

Only one thing stood in my way: me.

REMEMBER THE MOVIE
To begin restoring market share and brand love, I devised a marketing plan to connect with the local community. If we could give back to the community and give them a positive experience, we'd begin to improve Coke's reputation. *Brilliant!*

I contacted a local outdoor movie contractor, secured a venue a few miles north of town, and collaborated with the media team to develop an awareness campaign—radio commercials, in-store displays, and coolers with point of sale, and product sampling at the venue. We named the event "Sunset Cinema." Lastly, we needed to pick a movie to bring the community together. Ah-ha! "Remember the Titans." An inspirational message about unity, reaching one's potential, and overcoming the odds. A perfect match for the event and the cherry on top.

The plans were set, and I communicated them via email. That was my first mistake.

We needed a good showing to demonstrate that Coke and the local bottling team were back in the game. But a plan is only as good as its execution. Everything went differently than planned.

It rained that afternoon and into the evening of the event. When it rains, it pours.

We'd anticipated about 500 people at the event; only 25 showed up.

The media campaign started late and didn't have time to build awareness.

In-store displays and coolers with the point of sale weren't activated until the last minute.

The bottler's event team brought the wrong sampling product.

And that's not all.

Did you know that "Remember the Titans" prominently featured a certain beverage? I sure didn't. And can you guess which one? Yes, Pepsi. Our archrival ambushed a Coke event. I could see the team shaking their heads and even putting their faces in their hands.

So much for communicating by email.

I was livid, but on a deeper level, I was embarrassed and humiliated. All my grand career ambitions flashed before my eyes on their way to an early grave. So, I did what any competent professional would have done: I owned the disaster, apologized, and asked how to improve on the next one.

Not really. I did the exact opposite and went into CYA mode, acting like Louis Litt (Suits – IYKYK). I ripped into everyone I could find. I criticized the salespeople because they couldn't sell, and the operations team because they couldn't execute. I shouted at the promotions manager for not screening the movie before the event. I even called the media lead at home and expressed my disappointment. "Just do your damn job!" I yelled as I hung up on her.

It was all their fault.

BE KIND, REWIND

Then, the Market Unit Vice President approached me—my key stakeholder. If he wasn't happy, nobody was. I could see the disappointment on his face. He took a deep breath and said, "We didn't achieve our objective today, but it was a start." All my rage turned to shame.

"Preston, do you know what influence is?" he asked.

"Obviously not," I blurted. But I had a feeling he was going to tell me.

"Influence is leadership without the crutch of authority. You need to learn how to work *with* and *through* people to help turnaround this market; be a director not a dictator."

My defenses went back up.

"But that's what I thought I was doing. I developed a great plan and communicated it," I replied.

"It's not what you did. It's how you did it," he said.

Then, he explained that achieving a goal is one thing. How you get there, the manner in which you approach it, and the way you deal with people make all the difference. I needed everyone on the team to help accomplish our mission. Without them, there'd be no success.

In a low, 1930s-era gangster voice, he muttered, "Maybe you're the wrong guy for the job."

At that moment, I knew I'd soon be swimming with the fishes or losing my opportunity. The old ways of doing things, relying on myself, wouldn't work any longer. If it was to be, it was up to me to make a change—or be changed into another role, company, or opportunity.

The problem, the obstacle standing in the way of success, was me.

I was so focused on the *what*, I overlooked or even ignored the *how*.

The choice was clear: I could maintain my hard-charging, get-it-done mentality or learn how to become truly influential. I chose the latter, but I still had no idea how to get there.

This realization prompted a period of intense self-reflection, forcing me to confront the actual impact of my leadership style, how I treated others, and the priorities I had set for myself.

LOOKING IN THE MIRROR

Have you ever focused so much on results that you overlooked the people who help you achieve them?

Results matter. They are table stakes. You won't stick around long in any organization if you don't produce results. I've seen many managers or associates come in with great promise only to be forced out because they couldn't deliver on the objectives for which they were accountable. On the other hand, I've observed folks who delivered stellar results but left collateral damage in their wake. They put profits, processes, or projects over people.

Early in my career, I bought into the myth that focusing solely on achievements and outcomes was the key to success and fulfillment—in life and career. I was an awful manager and intolerable leader, but other than that, I was great at my job.

I'd gotten two degrees in business management, yet had no idea how to lead others.

I could manage projects and processes, but not people.

I could drive change, but drove people away.

I could manage tasks, but not teams.

I could develop plans, but struggled to execute them through individuals.

What was missing? The people aspect.

I always thought people were a means to an end. What end? My self-serving agenda – promotion, recognition, compensation. I never really considered people in my equation. I remember telling someone that "my performance would speak for itself regardless of the people damage I left in my wake."

Looking in the mirror that evening, I realized what I was doing wasn't working. Even more, it was self-destructive behavior. But the journey of a thousand miles starts with the first step. I asked, "What does *selflessness* look like?" and "Does it make a difference?"

THE TALE OF TWO CAPTAINS

Anytime I observe someone conveniently disappearing when work needs to be done, I call them the "Italian captain." The nickname comes from Francesco Schettino, the Costa Concordia's skipper. His ship wrecked, not in the middle of the ocean, but just off the coast of an Italian island. The disaster was caused by human error, killing 32 people and seriously injuring many more. Schettino blamed everyone but himself. To top it off, evidence suggests he abandoned the ship before the passengers and crew. He wasn't concerned for their safety and selfishly jumped into a lifeboat before others disembarked. Eventually, Schettino was found guilty of manslaughter, causing a shipwreck, getting off the boat before the passengers and crew (yes, that was a crime), and lying to authorities. He was sentenced to 16 years in prison.[1]

Contrast that with Captain Chesley Sullenberger. Piloting US Airways flight 1549 just after takeoff from New York City's LaGuardia Airport, the plane collided with a flock of geese. Both engines lost power, and "Sully" was forced to make an emergency landing in the Hudson River. The experienced pilot instructed the 150 passengers and five crew members to brace for impact. Immediately after the plane landed, Sully and the crew ushered passengers onto the wings to safety. As the plane was sinking, Sully went up and down the aisles twice to guarantee a complete evacuation before being the last to leave the aircraft. Sully was later honored by President Barack Obama for his heroic, selfless actions that led to the "Miracle on the Hudson."[2]

What do the captains have in common? They both abandoned ship. But *how* they did it differed significantly. We are drawn to selflessness and repelled by selfishness. The most destructive four-letter word in the English language is *self*. But it's our default—baked into our nature at some level. There must be a better way.

Just as the actions of Captains Schettino and Sullenberger illustrate the profound difference between selfishness and selflessness, I encountered a similar contrast in leadership styles during a pivotal meeting at work, much later in my career at Coke.

THE MEETING MAKEOVER

Ever get one of those meeting invites that feels a little fishy? The invitation subject line read, "Summer Promotion Planning Session." The purpose of the meeting was for directors like me to present our summer promotion plans to the Marketing Vice President, Edward. No other description or direction was provided.

While Edward was a brilliant and accomplished marketer, he had a reputation for being volatile, flying off the handle at any moment. He'd been known to verbally abuse his team when someone didn't know the answer to one of his questions or when work didn't meet his expectations. A number of my peers asked me why we were being summoned to the planning session. I told them I had no idea, but encouraged them to have their facts together; the meeting could be a rough one.

Because of a scheduling conflict, I attended the meeting virtually. I logged onto the meeting website and saw my peers sitting in the quiet room, looking apprehensive. Edward stormed into the room, sat down, and asked who wanted to go first. One poor soul raised their hand to volunteer.

Before the first presenter could say anything, Edward began peppering the individual with questions. His tone was condescending and became more intense as the dialogue progressed.

Finally, Edward stopped the individual mid-sentence and said, "Either you are incompetent, or you don't care. Which is it?"

I felt like I was watching a shark that smelled blood and began circling its prey.

After a long, uncomfortable pause, Edward said, "You obviously don't know your business. What are you worth? I ask again, either you are incompetent, or you don't care. Which is it?"

The first volunteer's face was bright red, and steam came from his ears. However, out of fear, he didn't respond.

Edward turned to the next person and demanded, "How about you? What are your summer promotion plans?" As the next person bravely began presenting, Edward pounced on the individual with pressing questions. The person became flustered and couldn't spit her words out. Edward sarcastically asked, "You too? Either you are incompetent, or you don't care about our business. Which is it?"

Edward then proceeded to ask everyone around the table the same question. When he finished, he stood up and announced, "I think I made my point. Everyone had better know their facts next time!" He stormed out of the room just as quickly as he entered. I was spared the berating because I attended virtually, and Edward didn't call on me.

I couldn't believe what I had just seen. The next day, I told my manager what had happened. He told me he'd already heard the negative feedback and assured me Edward's behavior would be addressed.

Then, I had a wild idea. *Meetings don't have to be like the one Edward just held. They can be productive, effective, and constructive while treating people with respect and dignity. Why don't I volunteer to lead the next plan presentation meeting and show there's a better way?*

I mentioned the idea to my manager. He paused and asked, "What will you do differently?"

"I'll let people know up front what's expected of them, create an environment where ideas can be exchanged, and feedback can be given."

My manager smiled and said, "I like it. Let's give it a try on our next go around."

I reached out to different VPs to align with my proposed format. I developed and provided a plan report template outlining expectations. Lastly, I facilitated a planning meeting with our cross-functional partners in a very positive environment.

I received great feedback, including a note from someone who also worked for Edward: " The plans shared today were excellent and definitely instilled confidence for success against this critical initiative. Thank you for all of the collaboration!"

There was a better way to achieve results: by treating people with dignity and respect. A positive and respectful culture isn't fluff or a "nice" thing to have; it's essential for effective teamwork and success.

THE LEADER'S IMPRINT: DISTINGUISHING YOURSELF WITH THE ART OF 'HOW'

To this day, those words, "It's not what you did, it's how you did it"—became my guiding principle.

Embracing the "how" doesn't just lead to successful results; it allows you to make a lasting, positive impact in your sphere of influence. It prepares you to be a leader who elevates others and transforms environments, not just accomplish goals.

Does this concept sound complicated? Or maybe too simplistic? It's both, as you'll see.

But where, or better yet, *how* do we begin? Starting points matter, too.

CHAPTER 1

Start with Who?

*"The key to success is sincerity.
If you can fake that, you've got it made."*
– GEORGE BURNS

Who doesn't love polar bears?

Okay, maybe seals and certain arctic inhabitants, but Coca-Cola and its customers sure love the combination. You've seen the ads.

There I was—not in the Arctic, but in the southeast US—in the thick of the food service world, overseeing Coca-Cola's "on-premise" operations. It was 2011, and the company was rolling out our big holiday campaign with those classic Santa and polar bear images on the cans. But this year, we wanted the imagery to stand for a good cause. The cans would have a new white design, celebrating our financial commitment to support polar bears and a wildlife refuge.

Over a billion cans were set to hit the market. *Cue the dramatic music.*

As the product rolled out, we started hearing rumbles of confusion, especially in healthcare, about this new can. Understandably, nurses mistook the white Coke can for Diet Coke, which had always worn a lighter-colored label. Imagine the chaos when a diabetic patient enjoyed a full-sugar Coke instead of a Diet Coke! It was a health fiasco waiting to happen.

Coke's brand identity is its rich, red hue—a beacon of tradition. But some zealous brand manager thought, "Let's shake things up!" Good intentions soon turned into a Coke and Mentos experiment gone wrong.

Consumers even started complaining that Coke in the white can tasted different. Perception's a powerful thing, huh? So, the company had to backtrack faster than a kid caught with their hand in the cookie jar. We pulled those white cans off the shelves, especially in hospitals, to squash the mix-up between Diet Coke and regular Coke.

This whole saga was a textbook case of mistaken identity.

Changing the look of the can, even for a noble cause, threw everyone off. It would be like me showing up at church wearing a neon orange suit—you'd think, *Who's this guy?* It wasn't just a packaging change, but a shake-up of Coca-Cola's deeply held essence.

Whether you're a global giant like Coca-Cola or just someone trying to make your mark, remember this: stay true to your *who*. Even when you're gunning for change and growth, don't lose sight of your core identity. In a world that's constantly changing, that's your anchor, your north star, your can of Coke in a sea of sodas.

WHO > WHY

You've probably been told to find your "Why"—that pulsing heartbeat of purpose that propels every step you take. But I'm going to ask you to join me in a different quest that digs a bit deeper into the soil of our very being: the quest for our "who."

Imagine a majestic and sturdy tree. Its strength isn't just in the beauty of its branches but in the unseen roots that anchor it firmly to the earth. Similarly, before we race towards the *why*, we need to be deeply rooted in the *who*—our character, values, innate strengths, peculiar quirks, and yes, the imperfections that make us uniquely ourselves— the very essence of our being.

Think about Coca-Cola for a moment. Before it's a product, it's a promise of nostalgia, consistent quality, and a taste that spans generations. That's it's *who*. And from there springs everything else—the marketing, the products, the global recognition. It's a classic example of "form before function," a crucial principle for us, too.

Now, I know Simon Sinek's "Start with Why" has become a mantra for inspiring businesses and individuals alike. It's powerful stuff, no doubt. But when it comes to the tapestry of our own lives, we're painting on a more personal canvas. It's not just about carving a space in the marketplace; it's about carving out our place in the world.

And that starts with who.

So, as we stand at the doorstep of this adventure, here's a tool that will light our way—the concentric circle diagram pictured on the following page. At the center is Identity, the core of your unique existence. It's only by knowing *who* you are that the "why" begins to make sense.

Wrapped around "Identity" is "Purpose," the driving force behind our actions and the core of what motivates us to act. Rooted within "Purpose" is "Meaning," the narratives we create about our lives and experiences that give context and significance to our actions. Then comes "Calling"—the inner voice that guides us to align our vocation with our abilities and transform our work into a significant contribution.

Beyond "Calling" are "Vision" and "Mission," and at the very edge, like the horizon, lies "Significance." This is where your story, illuminated by identity, purpose, and calling, painted with vision and mission, echoes into eternity.

Think of this book as a map. Each chapter is a step, and each concept is a landmark in your personal and professional growth.

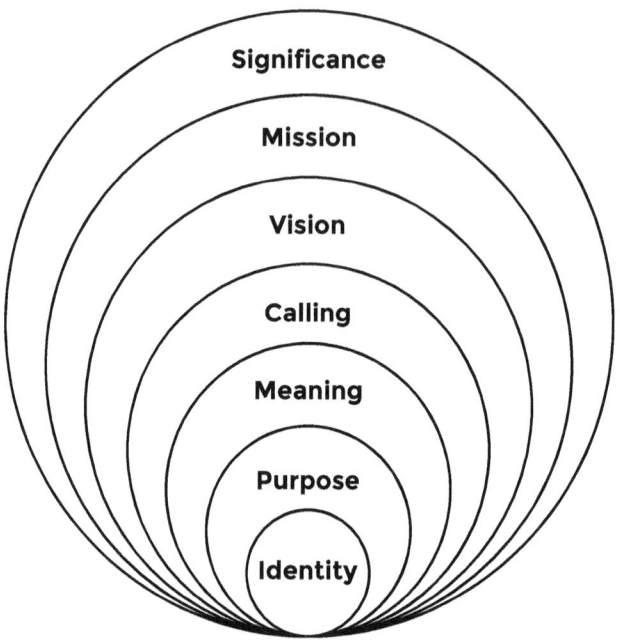

START STRONG: THE FOUNDATIONAL POWER OF IDENTITY IN SUCCESS

Imagine a coach who not only changed the game of basketball but also taught invaluable life lessons from the very first practice. That coach was John Wooden, UCLA Bruins Men's basketball head coach, the wizard of Westwood. His impressive record included ten national championships and being named NCAA College Basketball Coach of the Year *six* times[3]. Unprecedented indeed.

What underpinned this enduring success? It's how he started each season.

From day one, Coach Wooden taught his players the basics—and I'm not talking about layups or shooting drills. He taught them to put on their socks and shoes in a certain way. Why? Coach Wooden discovered that starting points matter. If a player's socks and shoes didn't fit well, they'd develop blisters or potentially twist an ankle.

Have you ever tried to play any sport with a foot blister? It's excruciating. You can't move or run at a normal pace. It slows you down. If you're on a team, you hinder their performance as well. You may miss practice or a game.

Like Coach Wooden's focus on the basics, identity is the starting point for your personal and professional growth. Understanding who you are—your beliefs, values, strengths, and experiences—guides your thoughts, choices, and actions. It shapes how you interact with the world and influences your sense of purpose. Get the foundation right, and everything can flourish from there.

FROM GREED TO GRACE

Picture a corporate prodigy. Mark Whitacre was the division president of a Fortune 500 company, living in a house that most people would never buy for themselves. He had the world by the tail. Or so it seemed. When I first met Mark, the man sitting before me was as different from the corporate titan as one could imagine. He had a story to tell, one that was twisty and turny and full of hard-won wisdom – and one that had come only after taking a long, hard, and honest look in a very particular mirror.

"I was on track to be CEO," Mark told me, his voice steady but laced with the kind of regret that comes from deep introspection. "I was making seven figures a year, but it was never about the money, not really. It was about winning, about being on top."

But here's the kicker: Mark's climb was not all that it seemed. "Under the mentorship of the CEO and president of ADM (Archer Daniels Midland), I would have stepped on my grandmother to achieve the next step up the ladder," he admitted. It's a shocking admission, a window into a world where the ends always justify the means.

At ADM, Mark found himself entangled in a price-fixing scandal, in which he and others conspired to manipulate the prices of lysine, a food additive. This illicit activity brought substantial financial gain for ADM and its executives. Still, it exacted a heavy personal and ethical toll. Burdened by the weight of his actions, Mark's conscience began to torment him, and he ultimately made the courageous decision to expose the corrupt practices at ADM.

Prompted by his wife, Mark's decision to cooperate with the FBI and become an informant came with its own challenges and risks. He wore a wire for several years, gathering evidence against his colleagues and superiors. Despite his cooperation, Mark also committed fraud by embezzling $9.5 million from ADM, leading to his indictment, nine-year sentence, and imprisonment.

On the day of his sentencing, "the judge scolded Mr. Whitacre for wasting a long list of advantages: a doctorate, a close family and a high-paying job. Saying Mr. Whitacre sometimes displayed 'sociopathic behavior,' Judge Baker said Mr. Whitacre was motivated by 'garden-variety venality and greed.'" [4]

As Mark described, the culture at ADM was one where intimidation reigned supreme. "They didn't care much about how they got anywhere. My job was not to be an advocate for my employees. It was just to get whatever I could out of my subordinates." This mindset paid off on the surface. The stock was doubling, and the executives' pockets were deepening, but at what cost?

For Mark, the cost was his conscience and sense of self. "Some of the things I did haunt me to this day," he said, shaking his head. I had a perfect opportunity to be a mentor, and instead, I tore people down, all in the name of success."

It's easy to see Mark's story as a parable about the pitfalls of hubris—a meteoric rise followed by a spectacular fall. But what I took away from my conversation with him was not just the fall but the redemption that came in the most unexpected place—prison.

"In prison, I came face-to-face with the fact that I'd miscalculated my life," Mark reflected. He learned that "it didn't matter what you earn, it matters how you do things and how you treat people." Stripped of his status, Mark found himself in a concrete cell, and it was there, ironically, that he began to rebuild his life on a more solid, authentic foundation.

Mark credits much of his transformation to a new mentor, Chuck Colson. A man who had his fall from grace during the Watergate Scandal, Colson's life had been transformed in prison, and he was helping others do the same through Prison Fellowship. Under Colson's guidance, Mark began to see life from a different perspective, but ultimately, his decision to surrender his life to Jesus Christ marked the turning point.

"For the first time, with Colson leading, I had a totally different trajectory," Mark said. "But it wasn't just his mentorship; it was the moment I surrendered my life to Jesus Christ that everything changed." He realized that his identity was not in his achievements but in who he was in Christ. "I really saw the life of significance," Mark explained. "It was so rewarding... not only to get results, but how I did it."

Helping his fellow inmates became Mark's new source of pride, a way to make amends and find meaning and purpose. When his friend TJ earned his GED and associate's degree, Mark found joy in his friend's success, a new and more fulfilling feeling than any corporate win.

The Mark Whitacre who emerged from prison was a man who understood the true value of who over why. "If you have a purpose in your life and your purpose is making the world a better place... you're gonna do life differently," he told me with a conviction that comes from living through the worst and finding a way to the other side. Even the Judge, prosecutor, and the FBI agents involved with the ADM/Mark Whitacre case became very supportive of Mark Whitacre years later as they observed his transformation while in prison.

Mark now shares his remarkable story with others. Even Hollywood got in on the action. His story has been seen by millions since it was the basis of the 2009 motion picture *The Informant*, starring Matt Damon as Mark.[5]

Here was a guy with all the trappings of success, yet his *who*—his core values and character—was out of sync with his *why*. His pursuit of purpose, skewed by a misguided sense of self, eventually led him down a path of self-destruction. It's a vivid illustration that when the who is compromised, no amount of why can set things right.

What, then, might we take away from Mark's story? The nature of our character, our values, and the difference we make to others is the foundation upon which a life of meaning can be built. It's not about the paycheck, the stock options, or the title; it's about the lives we touch, the people we elevate, and the legacy we choose to leave behind.

Remember Mark Whitacre's trajectory. Recall that, in the quest for professional glory, don't lose sight of what's important – namely, who you are and who you aspire to be. Because, after all, that's what makes you who you are, that's what carries you through the storms in the first place, and that's what matters most.

LASSO THE BS

Have you ever had a moment when you tried to project an image that wasn't real... and failed? I have.

In the journey of personal and professional growth, the essence of who you are—the core of your identity—plays a pivotal role. It's not just about the achievements you tally or the polished image you want to project; it's about the authenticity behind your actions and the integrity with which you conduct yourself. This is the heart of the How>What philosophy: the way you do things (how) is more important than what you do.

Based on circumstances early in my career, I sought a job change from the training industry back into consumer products. Why? The training role I had was exciting and glamorous at first. I was mentored and trained by some of the best in the industry to make crowd-pleasing presentations, sell dynamically, and exercise effective human relations skills. I often spoke at local civic clubs or non-profit organizations to polish my newly developed abilities and generate business leads. The role was fun, but I needed to pay the bills. With a young family and a baby daughter, I needed to find a more stable role.

Back in the day, jobs were posted in the newspaper's help-wanted ads. (For younger readers, feel free to search "what is a newspaper.") I looked at the paper every day for a new job opportunity. I saw a territory sales role with Hershey Chocolate. *Who doesn't like chocolate? I told myself that it should be an easier product to sell than training.* So, I sent my resume to the address in the ad and received an interview a few weeks later.

I prepped for the interview and thought it would be a slam dunk. With my consumer product sales experience, combined with my newly developed skills, I just knew I'd nail the interview.

Wanting to portray a polished image and look the part, I dressed in my best suit, tie, and shoes. I arrived at the hotel and stepped into the interview room. That's when I met Tom and Milt. Over a couple of hours, I successfully answered their questions, conveying my skill set and why I was an excellent fit for the role, and wooing them with my training background. They gave me buying signals, and I walked away from the interview confident that the job was mine.

The next day, I received the anticipated call for a second interview. I was so excited. I prepped just like I did for the first meeting. I remember walking into the hotel interview room and being again greeted by Tom and Milt. They asked the first question, and I went into presentation mode, mustering my training and skills to impress them.

"Preston," Tom interrupted. Lasso the bullshit!"

"Huh?" I thought.

Tom continued, "We believe you have all of the skills to be successful in our organization except one thing. You seem too polished, almost plastic. You communicate well, but you're not connecting with us. Your approach is inauthentic. To be successful with customers, you need to be real. And you seem a touch arrogant; it's all about you."

I was called out. Tom's comment cut to the quick and shook my soul. I had worked so hard to develop my skills and wanted to impress them during the interview. I needed the job so badly. *I've blown it.*

Tom said, "I'm not sure we want to continue, but I'll ask one last question… When's the last time you did something for someone else?"

I paused for what seemed like an eternity and began to sweat. *I'd better drop my guard and quit trying to portray a perfect image.*

Then, I told Tom and Milt about how my wife recently went through childbirth delivery complications and surgery. I shared how hard it was to see my wife incapacitated and the challenge of caring for our baby daughter in the midst of it all. My voice cracked as I told the story about serving my young family in a time of need. I was anything but polished. I took a risk and was vulnerable with Tom and Milt.

After hearing the story, Tom smiled and said, "That's what I was looking for. I was wondering if there was any humility inside of you. You are real, and customers will like you if you let the person we just saw out."

The great news is that I got the job and went on to be successful while at Hershey. I learned to be authentic and connect with customers. More importantly, Tom became a trusted mentor and friend over the years. I appreciated his challenge to be authentic.

Authenticity is the quality of being genuine. It's a critical building block of trust. Folks are attracted to someone who is real because they feel comfortable, safe, and respected. If people know and like you, they will believe you. So, how do you develop authenticity?

- Stop Pretending: People can sniff out inauthenticity. Be yourself, not what you think others want you to be. As the saying goes, "Be yourself; everyone else is taken."
- Let Your Guard Down: Vulnerability is the key to connecting with others. If you're open and honest with people, they will like and trust you.
- Quit Trying to Be Perfect: Don't be obsessed with your image or reputation. Embrace failures, brokenness, and hardships, and share how you've grown from your challenging experiences.

Do you struggle with authenticity? If so, how does it impact your relationships? Do you have trouble connecting with others? What would it look like if you stopped pretending, let your guard down, and quit trying to be perfect?

My challenge to you is to *lasso the bullshit*, and you'll become an authentic leader.

STAY REAL OR GET LOST

I've always laughed at the idea of authenticity. There's this notion floating around that authenticity means being whatever you feel like, declaring your identity, and reality be darned. Now, imagine me—Preston Poore, just your regular guy—proclaiming, "I feel like an astronaut today," despite my most adventurous journey being the daily commute.

It's like proclaiming myself a six-foot-nine-inch-tall female Chinese volleyball player when my style more resembles a Labrador

Retriever on the court. Or maybe announcing that I no longer owe a mortgage and am debt-free when I actually owe the bank money.

It's all in good fun until you realize some folks are serious. They're out there, identity-hopping like a game of musical chairs, and when the music stops, reality hits hard. That's not authenticity; that's a case of mistaken identity—and sometimes, not even a funny one.

Now, let's bring it back to something a bit closer to home: the Coca-Cola white can fiasco. They meant well, aiming to help polar bears and all, but ended up confusing the very people they aimed to serve. A classic mix-up, a slip in brand identity, and suddenly, the world's most recognizable drink is having an identity crisis. You could say Coke lost its "real" for a moment.

It's not about the label you slap on the outside but the truth of what's inside that counts. Just like Coke eventually realized, sometimes you've got to stick to your roots – because that's where the real magic happens.

Speaking of identity crises and staying true to your roots, let me share a personal story that illustrates how even the most trivial choices, like my sports fandom, can highlight the importance of understanding who you truly are.

TEAM LOYALTY? WHAT'S THAT?

I've been a lifelong fan of the Denver Broncos. Which is to say, I'm an aficionado of nostalgia. But when I transferred planes at DFW airport a few years ago, for reasons I can't even remember, I bought a Dallas Cowboys shirt. It wasn't a strategic decision. It was more like a spur-of-the-moment gesture of defiance. The Broncos' historic loss in their first Super Bowl was to the Cowboys, so maybe I just wanted to get on the enemy's team. My wife just rolls her eyes and calls it an #IdentityCrisis.

I've worn that Cowboys shirt around the world, and it's confirmed a hunch: those Cowboys are polarizing. No other team apparel I own sparks such passionate responses. In addition to the Cowboys shirt, I also own a Packers shirt, bought to accompany my single share of Green Bay Packers stock—a fun way to joke about being an NFL team owner.

People either love or hate "them Cowboys." In Paris, someone yelled, "The Cowboys suck!" while I was wearing the shirt. In Peru, someone shouted, "Go Cowboys!" And on a recent tour in the Middle East, I wore the shirt, prompting the tour leader—a die-hard Chicago Bears fan—to shake his head at me. The next day, I wore my Green Bay Packers shirt, and he did a double-take, saying, "What the…?" I explained that I'd once purchased one share of Packers stock, and he just looked at me and said, "Dude, you've got an identity problem."

He could be right. But most of us have a "who" problem, especially at work. The path begins with knowing not what you do, where you came from, or what you have, but who you are—your values, character, strengths, and weaknesses.

In the world of professional growth and personal development, it's easy to get caught up in the "what"—the job titles, the accolades, the external markers of success. But true fulfillment and effective leadership come from understanding and embracing your "who." This is the core of the How>What philosophy: the way you do things (How) is more important than the actions themselves (What). Your identity—your authentic self—should guide your actions and decisions.

So, while I may have an identity crisis regarding football fandom, it's a humorous reminder of a more profound truth. Just as I juggle my allegiances between the Broncos, Cowboys, and Packers, we all navigate various aspects of our identities in our professional lives. The key is to stay true to who you are at the core. Embrace your unique character, strengths, and weaknesses because that will ultimately guide *how* you lead and contribute.

Go Broncos! Wait, *Go, Pack, Go!* Hold on, *Go Cowboys!* Oh well. See what I mean?

PRINCIPLE
Know Your Core

QUESTIONS

Your identity is "who you are, the way you think about yourself, the way you are viewed by the world, and the characteristics that define you."

What forms your identity—your sense of self? Psychology Today says, "Identity formation involves three key tasks: discovering and developing one's potential, choosing one's purpose in life, and finding opportunities to exercise that potential and purpose. Identity is also influenced by parents and peers during childhood and experimentation in adolescence."[6]

What three words describe some key elements of your unique personality?

_____

_____

_____

We should not form our identity based on others' feedback, but their perspective can be an excellent measure of how much we live from our authentic selves. We are all a work in progress, after all. Who do others say you are?

_____

_____

_____

CHAPTER 2

Driving with Purpose

"The difference between stupidity and
genius is that genius has its limits."
— ALBERT EINSTEIN

College was a transformative period for me. I went from being that 5'2" kid in junior high—often the target of bullies—to a 6'1" 190-pound young man. I lifted weights and crafted an image of intimidation to fend off potential bullies. It was my way of compensating for the insecurities and struggles of my earlier years.

I began my college journey at the University of Colorado, infamous at the time as the #1 party school in the nation. It was there that I lost my way. I began drinking heavily—once consuming a liter of rum in just two hours, which turned into a night that nearly ended in tragedy. Despite the close call, I continued down this destructive path, turning my back on my faith and embracing a lifestyle far from what I knew to be right.

My grades plummeted, and I eventually had to leave CU, returning home to attend Colorado State University. Living in my parents' basement, I sought solace and social validation by joining Sigma Chi. I surrounded myself with the coolest, toughest guys, still trying to prove I was no longer that bullied kid from junior high.

At CSU, I dated a girl from high school who epitomized everything I aspired to be—popular, athletic, and successful. But I was devastated when she broke up with me during our senior year. I felt worthless, having placed all my self-worth in her approval. One night, in my despair, I drank heavily and ended up vomiting on my Bible. That moment was a vivid wake-up call. I realized how far I had strayed from my faith and values.

Being broken and depressed, I needed a fresh start. After graduation, I moved to Birmingham, Alabama, where my extended family lived, seeking to rediscover my identity and find my purpose. As I drove away from Colorado, "Sweet Home Alabama" played on the radio. It felt like a sign, a wink toward the new chapter of my life. I found an unaccustomed confidence that I wasn't just running away but searching for something more profound—my purpose, meaning, and calling.

I know what it's like to wrestle with those existential questions. *Who am I? Why am I here? Do I matter? What's the meaning of life?*

Through these trials, I discovered that purpose isn't found in validation from others or the pursuit of fleeting pleasures. It's found in aligning with a greater plan, understanding that we are known and planned for long before our birth. This journey has shaped me, leading me to contribute positively to the world and cherish the precious gift of life.

I don't have it all figured out, but I've learned a lot along the way. In fact, I have a PhD from the School of Hard Knocks. Life is both a journey and a destination. It's not only about what you do but also how you do it—embracing the How>What philosophy. Pursuing purpose, meaning, and calling is a worthy endeavor.

Sadly, this struggle with purpose is not unique to me; it's a widespread epidemic.

CHASING HAPPINESS, FINDING EMPTINESS

A whopping eighty-four percent of Americans believe the highest goal of life is enjoying yourself.[7] Since so many people seem to be pursuing that goal, our overall enjoyment of life should be increasing. But the opposite appears to be true.

- Harvard University reports, "Nearly 3 in 5 young adults, 18 to 25 year olds[8], (58%) reported that they lacked 'meaning or purpose' in their lives in the previous month. Half of young adults reported that their mental health was negatively influenced by 'not knowing what to do with my life.'"[9]
- "An estimated 21.0 million adults in the United States had at least one major depressive episode. This number represented 8.3% of all U.S. adults. The prevalence of adults with a major depressive episode was highest among individuals aged 18-25 (18.6%)."[10]
- "Provisional CDC data shows that the number of suicide deaths in 2022 is the highest recorded, exceeding the next closest year (2018) by over 1,000 deaths. When adjusted for population growth and age, the suicide rate has risen by 16% from 2011 to 2022."[11]
- "[CDC] data suggests suicides are more common in the U.S. than at any time since the dawn of World War II."[12]

To borrow a word from my friend, *Yikes!* So, if answering "how" is the most important step to a thriving life and career, where do we begin? We can find purpose, meaning, and calling by pointing toward something bigger than ourselves.

PURPOSE, MEANING, CALLING: LIFE'S PERFECT TRIO
Let's begin with some definitions.

Purpose is your why—the overarching direction or intention that guides our life decisions and actions. It provides a sense of direction and can evolve with our experiences and life stages. Purpose is broad and all-encompassing, setting the course for how we live our lives. It's our why.

Meaning in life is often associated with the value we ascribe to our experiences and existence. It makes our lives feel worthwhile and can be derived from various aspects, not limited to work. Meaning brings depth; it yields a sense of fulfillment, satisfaction, and impact. It's what's worthwhile.

Calling is a more specific term, often described as a strong inner impulse toward a particular action or vocation that aligns with one's passions. It is how we actualize our purpose. It's a "street view" of our purpose. While purpose gives our life direction and motivation, calling is the personal pursuit of that purpose. It's important to note that calling can change over time during different seasons of life. Ultimately, calling is about finding and fulfilling our distinctive role in the world. It's our work.

With a clear sense of purpose, we can explore what brings meaning to our lives. Our calling becomes the tangible expression of this purpose, manifesting through our careers, service to others, or other fulfilling endeavors. When purpose, meaning, and calling align, it transforms our outlook. Imagine waking up each day enthusiastically, thinking, "Thank God it's morning!" instead of dragging yourself out of bed with a groan, "Oh God, it's morning." Our outlook drives our outcomes, and aligning these elements sets the stage for a fulfilling and impactful life.

Ultimately, the ideal sequence might look like this: start with self-understanding (identity), use this insight to define your overarching purpose, explore what aspects of life bring you meaning, and from there, identify your calling—the specific ways you can live out that purpose and meaning.

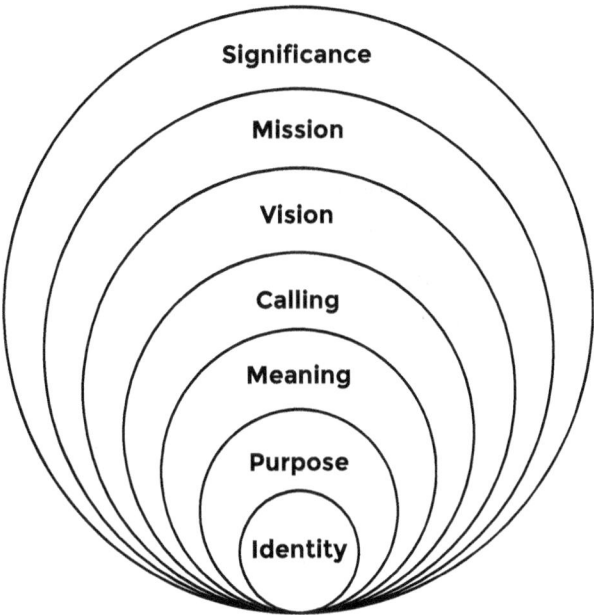

PURPOSE PACKAGED, MEANING POURED, CALLING PURSUED

Imagine an 8-oz. glass bottle of ice-cold Coca-Cola – my favorite way to enjoy a Coke.

The design and branding of the Coca-Cola bottle represent purpose. Its iconic contour shape, red label, and Spencerian script guide consumers to choose it, providing clear direction in a sea of countless options. This purpose (*why*) sets the course for how the product stands out in the marketplace.

The beverage inside the bottle is more than just a drink; it symbolizes refreshment and enjoyment. It's a testament to the brand's purpose, offering satisfaction and delight—emotional refreshment, as my mentor called it. It symbolizes the meaning (*worthwhile*) we derive from understanding and embracing our values and experiences.

The role of the Coca-Cola brand team and producers represents calling—maintaining the brand's reputation as a beloved choice for consumers worldwide (*work*).

The Coca-Cola bottle analogy demonstrates how purpose, meaning, and calling synergistically shape our lives. Like the bottle's design, purpose provides us with a clear path. Meaning, like the refreshing beverage inside adds satisfaction. Calling, mirrored in the dedication of Coca-Cola's brand team and producers, fuels our passion. This approach can lead to long-term impact, much like Coca-Cola's global influence.

Drifting, Empty, and Flat: Life without Direction

So, for a moment, let's consider what life looks like without purpose, meaning, and calling. Without purpose, our lives can become aimless, lacking direction and focus. It's like a plain bottle without its thoughtful design—it blends into the background, unnoticed and unremarkable. A life without purpose drifts without a clear path.

When we lack meaning, our experiences and efforts can feel worthless, devoid of fulfillment and significance. It's like a beverage that fails to refresh, satisfy, or energize, leaving us empty.

Lastly, we miss out on our distinctive role in life without a calling. Our roles and contributions can turn into drudgery—just going through the motions without passion or joy. Imagine the Coca-Cola brand team working without dedication, resulting in a product that doesn't resonate with consumers. It falls flat.

Understanding these contrasts highlights the importance of purpose, meaning, and calling in our lives. By aligning our life's compass with these principles, we can navigate our journey with direction, value, and passion.

ROLES THAT DEFINE AND DRIVE US

We take on various roles that reflect our identity and values in life. These roles help us explore and express our purpose (*why*), find meaning (*worthwhile*), and fulfill our calling (*work*). By understanding how these elements interact, we can lead successful and deeply fulfilling lives.

For example, one of my roles in life is author. My purpose (*why*) is to create and share stories, concepts, or principles that educate, equip, and inspire others. Writing is meaningful (*worthwhile*) to me because I find joy in the creative process and the impact of written words on readers. My calling is to use my writing talents (*work*) to convey messages and connect with an audience.

While at Coke, one of my roles was a people manager. My purpose was to lead and develop a team (*why*), fostering a productive and positive work environment. I derived a sense of accomplishment from seeing team members grow and succeed (worthwhile). My calling was to utilize my leadership abilities to mentor and guide employees (work), ensuring they reach their potential and contribute to the company's success.

Another was parenting. My purpose (why) was to nurture, protect, and guide my children, ensuring they grow into responsible, kind, and capable individuals. I found meaning in the daily acts of parenting (*worthwhile*), from eating dinner together and helping coach sports teams to celebrating milestones and encouraging my kids during tough times. My calling was to embrace the role of a parent with dedication and love (work), using personal strengths and instincts to foster a supportive and loving environment that helped my children thrive.

Purpose, meaning, and calling are practical drivers that shape our actions and influence our lives. Recognizing and embracing these dimensions in our roles allows us to navigate life with clarity and passion. By fulfilling these roles, we enrich our lives and positively impact those around us.

RALLYING FOR A CAUSE

My friend Dean Crowe's journey started with a profoundly moving experience involving William, a young boy battling cancer. This moment ignited her purpose: to make a significant impact on the lives of children with cancer. She realized that "simply making dinner" for someone wasn't enough to address the severe needs these children and families faced.

When William relapsed, Dean told me she felt an overwhelming urge to visit him in the hospital "despite having a turkey in the oven." This visit opened her eyes to the dire challenges faced by children with cancer. Dean asked William's mother, Nancy, what she could do. Without hesitation, Nancy replied, "raise money for childhood cancer research," highlighting the significant funding gap compared to adult cancer research. This pivotal conversation made her realize that providing meals wasn't meaningful to her, but actions that produced tangible financial results were meaningful.

Leveraging her investigative skills, Dean described to me how she uncovered the truth about the lack of funding for childhood cancer research, with validation from a CNN investigator. This fueled her determination to tackle the issue head-on. Dean founded the Rally Foundation based on her calling: to raise awareness and funds for childhood cancer research, focusing on high-risk, high-reward projects that larger organizations often overlooked.

Since its founding in 2005, the Rally Foundation has funded over $35 million in childhood cancer research grants, which in turn have supported 597 projects at hospitals and institutions across the country and worldwide. In 2024, Rally distributed a record $5 million in grants to 74 researchers at 34 institutions, the largest grant distribution in its history. The financial backing from Rally opens the door for cutting-edge research that paves the way for new treatments and better outcomes for children in the fight against cancer.[13]

Her enthusiasm inspired donors and galvanized those who had a vested interest in ensuring the children's success. Meanwhile, Rally-funded studies had already led to a cure for one form of leukemia and, beyond that, new and improved treatments for children with cancer – including CAR-T cell therapy to treat Acute Lymphoblastic Leukemia (ALL) and engineered antibodies for Neuroblastoma.

Dean's journey is a prime example of the How>What philosophy. Her purpose wasn't an abstract concept; it was a guiding force that shaped her actions. It gave her efforts meaning and direction. By living out her purpose, Dean not only found fulfillment but also made a profound impact on the lives of countless children and families. Her story shows just how powerful life can be when we're driven by a clear and compelling "why."

IT MAKES MY HEART SING

Meaning is profoundly personal. It's not something you can borrow or mimic; it emerges from the essence of who you are and what you stand for. Meaning surpasses the fleeting satisfaction of success or happiness. It's found in the fabric of your passions, values, creativity—and even in your struggles. Individual meaning may be found in others (family, spouse, friends), what you do (career, retirement, hobbies, travel, education, service), or the bigger picture (institutions, nature, faith).[14]

If purpose is an action-oriented concept, then meaning is an understanding-oriented concept.

Have you ever tuned in to 'American Idol'? I've been a fan since its inception, drawn not just to the voices but to the personal odysseys behind them. There's a moment I relish—when the wisdom of a mentor unlocks a contestant's hidden potential, and suddenly, they're not just singing notes; they're telling their story, their performance soaring to new heights. That moment gets me every time; it's when my heart sings, too.

Why does this matter to me? Well, it's much like the fulfillment I feel when someone I've coached leaps forward. It's a visceral reaction — a blend of pride and excitement- telling me my efforts have mattered in someone else's journey. It's deeply satisfying and full of *meaning:* meaningful.

MORE THAN MARKETING: FINDING MEANING AT COKE

A mentor once told me, "I can't imagine anything less important or relevant than how many people drink Coke instead of Pepsi."

This reminds me of the famous conversation Steve Jobs had with Pepsi CEO John Scully. Steve was courting John to come work for Apple. Steve famously said, "Do you want to sell sugar water for the rest of your life, or do you want to come with me and change the world?" Sculley moved to Apple and failed miserably. [15]

Contrast Jobs' statement with The Coca-Cola Company's purpose statement, "To refresh the world and make a difference."[16]

When I read those words, my sense of meaning resonated with the Company's purpose, and I decided I wanted to align myself with that meaningful work. My purpose, inside the company's purpose, was to create an environment where people could flourish, where they would be appreciated, valued, trusted, cared for, developed, and promoted.

Working at Coke wasn't a bed of roses. Many tasks and roles brought no sense of meaning or purpose. The mundane was always on the agenda. For example, I called myself the CPO (Chief Point-of-Sale Officer). Why? Someone had to determine how many pole signs, shelf talkers, static clings, barrels, and displays needed to be ordered for each store. A tedious and repetitive process. The algorithm I developed saved time and money for our bottling partners. Guess what? The model was so effective that I was put in charge of managing it. I found myself in front of a computer, working with spreadsheets more than I wanted. It was like chewing cardboard. Boring!

A few years later, things changed, thankfully. I reported to a new senior vice president over our franchise leadership organization, which worked with our bottling partners. We had sixty-eight bottling partners, and our jobs required us to work with them to ensure we were aligned on strategies and then inspire excellent execution.

To accomplish this, we had a tool called the System Alignment Model (SAM). The Model was a two-day organizational effectiveness workshop originally designed to facilitate new Company or bottler leadership changes, heal damaged relationships, or transform teams from good to great. It required the Company and bottling partner executive leadership to attend the workshop and identify challenges and solutions.

Why is System (i.e., The Coca-Cola Company and its Bottling Partners) alignment important? Each is an independent entity, a separate business, yet reliant on one another. Symbiotic. One can't be successful without the other. The Coke Company can market great brands all day, but no one wins if the bottling partners don't execute well. And vice versa, if the bottling partners execute well but The Coke Company doesn't generate demand, it's a recipe for disaster – products sit on the shelf. Alignment is key. No other consumer products organization is stronger than when The Coca-Cola Company and its bottling partners are aligned; nothing can stop them.

One day, the SVP pulled me aside and said, "Would you be interested in retooling, reinvigorating, and refreshing the System Alignment Model. You like meaningful work like that, right?" You bet I did. While SAM was a needed tool in the world of franchise and franchisee relationships, the Model and methodology became stale.

The SVP recognized that I loved working with people to shape, improve, and refresh teams and organizations. But reshaping that model was not going to be easy, yet it would be meaningful because there was a huge opportunity to help people more than just selling sugar water.

Over the next year, I collaborated with several key stakeholders from all over the world of Coca-Cola. We developed a workshop that included a diagnostic survey to determine alignment levels. Then, the survey results were reviewed in the workshop, showing opportunity areas. Next, we leveraged workshop tools that led to shared values, legacy statements, ways of working, operating model alignment, and creating a joint definition of winning. The workshop also helped define roles and responsibilities, what great execution looked like, common goals, metrics, and scorecards, and how both entities made money.

It was an eye-opening experience, for sure.

The workshop was renamed "Partnering for Growth," and we were off to the races. The workshop was conducted worldwide with a new friend and facilitator from Ireland supporting our efforts. By the way, I never told anyone this, but the acronym for Partnering for Growth was P4G. If you hit the shift key when typing "4," it will change to P$G. Notice the dollar sign? I always consider the workshop more than a feel-good exercise that some in leadership thought, but one that resulted in revenue and profit growth because of the System alignment created.

Many Coca-Cola Company and Bottling Partner relationships went from broken, combative engagements to ones where they became valued partners. Other workshops resulted in accelerated leadership changes or taking business and collaboration to another level.

For example, the workshop restored a broken relationship between the Coke Company and its bottling partner in Canada. They were barely talking to each other. In fact, the bottling partner was so frustrated that they stopped paying their concentrate invoices that were due to Coke. After helping to restore trust during the workshop and opening dialogue between the two entities, payments were resumed, and the workshop participants created a plan to move forward together, resolving their differences.

That's one example of many. It was meaningful work, worthwhile, and it made my heart sing. By focusing on purpose and how I led, I turned mundane tasks into meaningful work.

WHEN CALLS MATTER MORE THAN CAREERS

A telephone on the wall. The Yellow Pages. Answering machines. Even the word "telephone" shows my age. It's just a phone now, of course. There are over 8 billion smartphones and only 7 billion people on the planet.[17] It's like some people want a phone in each hand. Closer to home, did you know that Atlanta has the highest call volume per capita?[18] Now, I understand what we're doing during our lengthy commutes.

Texting has become our primary mobile communication method. An astonishing 19 billion texts are sent daily.[19] And hopefully, you're not texting while driving, especially if you have two phones.

I call my mom and dad every Sunday evening – a tradition we've held for almost thirty-five years. When we FaceTime with my father-in-law, we enjoy looking at his ear. He still hasn't figured out the video call thing.

When we were dating, I spent hours on the phone talking to my wife, Carla. Now, it's usually a brief call: "I'm headed to the grocery store. Do you need anything?" Some things change, but some never will. Whether it's a phone call, text, or FaceTime, all calls require a caller and a callee.

That takes me back to the word "telephone." Did you know the Greek "translation" for telephone is "distant voice"? The first distant voice heard over a telephone said, "Mr. Watson, come here. I want to see you." Were Alexander Graham Bell's words to his assistant the first voice-to-voice call? Maybe. But through a different "technology," one of the first distant voice calls was from a burning bush.

The book of Exodus, Chapter 3, reads: "And the angel of the Lord appeared to him in a flame of fire out of the midst of a bush. He looked, and behold, the bush was burning, yet it was not consumed. And Moses said, 'I will turn aside to see this great sight, why the bush is not burned.' When the Lord saw that he turned aside to see, God called to him out of the bush, 'Moses, Moses!' And he said, 'Here I am.'"

You know the rest of the story. It all started with that call.

What happens when you hear a call but can't confirm it's the right thing, the right timing, the right opportunity? That's where I found myself in 2010.

I was in the midst of another Coca-Cola organizational change. By the way, I survived eleven reorganizations during my twenty-plus-year tenure. This reorg found me without a position in Knoxville, where we'd lived for eight years, and required us to relocate to Atlanta. We were blessed with a wonderful church family where I served as an elder and was passionate about helping others grow in their faith. Our family didn't want to leave East Tennessee. My Pastor at the time, knowing of our predicament, invited me to lunch a couple of weeks before relocating. He shared his vision for the church, drew out an organization chart, showed me the role he had in mind, and said with almost a roar, "This might be your burning bush moment!"

His offer humbled me. I went home and told Carla about the opportunity. We prayed, played out all of the scenarios, and prayed again. The decision process was heart-wrenching. We wanted to stay in Knoxville, but something wasn't right. Was it the right opportunity? Maybe. Was it a stretch role that leveraged my gifts and skills? Yes. But I never felt a burning passion in my heart for the new role at church and wasn't inspired to make a radical career change.

So, I turned down the opportunity. I chose to stay in the marketplace and not enter the ministry. I've often wondered what would have happened if I had taken the role. Life is messy, but I believe God engineers our path based on our calling. And while there are always "What ifs," it's been made clear to me that I made the right choice based on understanding purpose, meaning, and calling.

But how do you determine your calling—your life mission, something you feel deeply drawn to and are passionate about? That which encompasses a sense of purpose and meaning that goes beyond merely making a living?

First, look around you. What story do you find yourself a part of?

Next, ask: Is there good? Celebrate and protect it. Is something missing? Fill the gap. Is something immoral or unethical? Oppose and change it. Is something broken? Restore it.

I'm glad I didn't accept the call to go into the ministry because I felt called to make Coke a great place to work. I found myself part of a Fortune 100 company with plenty of opportunities to make a positive difference.

Where good work was done, I recognized it and encouraged others. When someone was needed to do a demanding task, I volunteered (or was volun*told*) for it. When there was injustice in the workplace or low morale, I worked to change it. If something wasn't functioning, I helped fix the problem. My calling was to be a redemptive influence in the workplace, to make things better even though we were "just selling sugar water."

I never encountered a burning bush, but the passion to make the workplace great burned within me. It gave me purpose, was meaningful, and allowed me to answer my calling to make a positive difference.

THE HEART OF THE JOURNEY: CONNECTING PURPOSE, MEANING, AND CALLING

I've come to see life as a gift—one with purpose, meaning, and calling. I want to make the most of it. To somehow contribute to this chaotic world. Shape it. Improve it. Refresh it. I've been blessed with a loving mother, a nurturing father, the friendship of a brother, and caring in-laws. I married my Scarlett O'Hara (think *Gone with the Wind*)—a woman as beautiful and spirited as she is resilient and loving. My children are the apple of my eye.

Reflecting on my journey, I realize how far I've come from being a little kid in Colorado to walking the streets of Moscow, Istanbul, or Lima. Watching a Key West sunset, riding a camel in Tunisia, biking through Europe, or enjoying roller coasters at Universal Studios—these experiences have shown me the preciousness of life. It hasn't always been easy, but it's been good.

From my transformative college experiences to my career at Coca-Cola and Dean Crowe's passionate advocacy with the Rally Foundation, each narrative underscores a vital truth: how we approach our journey defines our ultimate impact. It's not just about the goals we achieve but the calling we answer. As you reflect on these stories, consider your path, and let the "how" guide you to a meaningful and purposeful "what." Live your calling, stay true to your journey, and let your heart sing.

PRINCIPLE
Drive with purpose

QUESTIONS

Based on your understanding of your identity, as we covered in Chapter 1, how would you describe your overarching purpose? (You don't have to feel like you have it all figured out. Plant a flag and navigate from there!)

_____
_____
_____

As you reflect on your life in this context, what aspects of life bring a sense of meaning?

_____
_____
_____

Based on your answers above, there will be signs that point to your calling—specific areas you're drawn to. Write a few down.

_____
_____
_____

CHAPTER 3

The Mission of Vision

"To the person who does not know where he wants to go, there is no favorable wind."

– SENECA

Without a clear vision, teams fall into chaos. Or, more accurately, the chaos *inside* the leader soon permeates the team.

Soon after a merger between two large organizations, our newly formed group was infected with infighting and chaos. I recall one group member consistently stirring the pot, continually criticizing our manager, team, and work. She never provided solutions. When something went wrong, she would "dog pile"—jumping in to add complaints and negativity to the challenge and making it worse.

Her attitude began to spread, just like what happens when you put an apple and an onion next to each other in the refrigerator. The apple, although initially sweet, will begin to taste like the bitter onion if they are left together long enough. Before long, everyone began pursuing selfish agendas and jockeying for positions, which resulted in a non-cooperative group. It stunk.

We also suffered a credibility gap with our internal client. The new group wasn't sure of our role and how we added value to the business. Our lack of clarity became a dense fog in our client's eyes.

I was very uncomfortable with our circumstances. And to make matters worse, I found myself bombarded with critical thoughts and was tempted to join in the negativity. Then I remembered what Solomon said, "Where there is no *vision*, the people will perish." (Proverbs 29:18 KJV). Meaning that people will experience chaos, division, unproductiveness, and scatter without vision. If there is a clear idea of a preferred future, people will unify with direction, passion, and a focused mindset. They will experience the hope of a better tomorrow and accomplish great things. That's the huge power of a simple vision.

Like King Solomon, I prayed that God would grant me wisdom and the ability to positively influence the team. During a one-on-one meeting with my manager, I asked him if he had a vision for the group, what he wanted to accomplish, and his plans to make the vision a reality. After a dramatic pause, he responded with a simple "Nope." This confirmed what I could clearly see – without vision, our team would never be productive, helpful, or considered our clients' strategic partners.

We discussed the challenges the newly formed group was facing. I shared with him that I had a burning desire to make our new organization and the team a great place to work. To help be part of the solution, I asked if I could contribute to developing a team vision and mission statement – articulating who we want to become, creating an idea of our preferred future, and planning how we'd get there.

"I'm no good at vision stuff and not sure it will help," he said. "But I'm fully supportive if you can help me turn the ship around."

Over the next few weeks, I connected with my peers and asked them what was on their hearts and minds about the team. I wondered if they saw the same challenges and problems that I did. Then, I asked them what they wanted to become as a group. (That's the vision part.) They all told me that they wanted to become a collaborative team, be valued as strategic partners, make a positive difference, and deliver strong business results.

Based on their thoughts, we (that's the *how* part: *we*) crafted the below vision/mission statement:

"To win the hearts of our teammates, customers, and consumers and positively influence our company's future by:

- MOLDING world-class commercial strategies through distinguished collaboration
- ENABLING exceptional execution that delivers winning results
- BUILDING an authentic team that trusts one another and takes pride in its work
- NURTURING and equipping our people to lead in the future
- CELEBRATING wins frequently to build momentum

Our vision and mission statement wasn't just a paper tiger—it was a guiding force that shaped everything we did. The vision came to life through our collective efforts (think mission), as each team member embraced it fully and made it their own. I'll never forget the stories shared by our staff, recounting how the vision manifested in their work and with their stakeholders. It wasn't something we merely talked about; it was something we lived and breathed.

We MOLDED national promotions (e.g., NCAA, Olympics, Holidays) by adding value rather than just passing along what was given to us. Through close collaboration with our stakeholders, we made sure our campaigns were customized for our local markets, as opposed to phoning in a cookie-cutter promo.

We ENABLED exceptional execution by planning and clearly communicating every promotion or new product launch. The how—listening to make sure every team member fully understood their role, priorities, and tools.

We BUILT a unified team by developing shared goals and being the first to extend trust to one another. Through open communication and self-disclosure, we fostered an environment where collaboration thrived. The *how*—enjoying trust and shared purpose—was more valuable than what we achieved. The way we prioritized relationships over mere outcomes led to extraordinary results.

We NURTURED our people by expecting them to take control of their growth and influence. We ensured that future leaders could thrive by fostering a culture that prioritized accountability and personal development.

We CELEBRATED by publicly acknowledging small wins and giving credit where it was due. The *how*—building loyalty and momentum through genuine appreciation—strengthened our morale and reinforced our collaborative spirit.

Our success didn't come from putting our vision and mission in a beautiful frame and hanging it on a wall. (We didn't even do that.) It came from how we lived them out every day.

As we brought this vision and mission to life, other regions noticed and sought to understand how we achieved such remarkable results. We openly shared our processes and the deliberate ways we infused the vision into our daily work. This recognition was significant for our team, affirming how we truly made a difference.

Vision Done Right: 8 Steps to Success

Despite the eye-rolling experiences most of us have had with vision statements, having a clear vision and writing it down is crucial to the health of your organization. As described above, I developed a clear vision statement by following this process.

1. **Look within and write it out.** My passionate desire was to make our team a destination—a great place to work where people thrived, produced superior results, and found meaning in their careers. I envisioned a future where we were a collaborative team and considered an indispensable business partner.

2. **Take ownership and act.** I approached my manager and asked if I could help. I intentionally volunteered so I could shape our team's future.
3. **Define the problem—with brutal honesty.** Our division and unproductiveness were a result of having no vision: we didn't know who we wanted to be, what we wanted to be known for, or what we wanted to accomplish.
4. **Collaborate for a solution.** Listen to others, seek common ground, and agree about where you want to go. This creates a shared vision.
5. **Identify WIIFM (What's in It for Me?).** For people to truly embrace a vision, they need to see how it benefits them personally and professionally. A vision that resonates on a personal level becomes a shared dream. Help your team see how realizing the vision not only elevates the organization but also advances their individual growth and success.
6. **Write it down.** Use the formula "To [contribution/goal], so that [impact]. Using our vision statement as an example: "To win the hearts and minds of our teammates, customers, and consumers [contribution/goal] so that we positively influence our company's future [impact]. Read on to discover how to write a mission statement.
7. **Gain commitment from your team.** Effective visions are written on the hearts and minds of people, especially if they are *asked* for their input and commitment. So when you ask, listen, and model collaboration at the outset.
8. **Tell stories.** Every week, share examples of how the vision is being brought to life – allowing the team to refer back to the bigger picture. This simple act moves the words written on a page to being written on the heart.

By following these steps, with emphasis on *how* you follow them, you can create a vision that not only guides but also transforms your team.

FROM THE FRONT LINES TO THE FRONT OFFICE: A MISSION OF IMPACT

Tom Stuper grew up in Austinburg, Ohio, and later joined the Army in 2008, seeking to pursue a meaningful career. Despite initial medical rejections due to flat feet, he was accepted amid the heightened enlistment period following 9/11. Tom served as an intelligence analyst with the 5th Squadron, 4th Cavalry Regiment, deploying to Iraq in 2009. His role involved tracking operations, working closely with Special Forces and intelligence units to capture high-value targets and ensure operational security.

In 2011, during his deployment in Baghdad, stationed at Victory Base Complex Joint Operations (VBC), Tom and his unit were responsible for setting up communications and office spaces for incoming troops. One day, they were moving equipment from shipping containers when the base's Phalanx system, a ground-based missile defense adapted from naval technology, intercepted an improvised rocket-assisted mortar (IRAM) aimed at the location. The IRAM, a deadly makeshift missile loaded with explosives and shrapnel, would have caused significant casualties if not intercepted.

Tom vividly recalls that day: "We were just milling around, moving equipment, when suddenly I heard the spray of bullets from the Phalanx system. I looked up and saw a large explosion in the air. It took a moment to realize what had happened. The missile was coming straight for us, and the system intercepted it just in time. It was terrifying and surreal."

The experience profoundly impacted Tom, reinforcing his belief in the importance of advanced defense technologies. "I fervently believe that the Phalanx system saved my life that day. I think about it often, especially when I see the work we do at Numerica," he said years later.

After leaving the Army in 2013 and pursuing further education, Tom eventually joined Numerica Corporation in 2018. When Tom discovered Numerica's mission- 'Driven by a pioneering spirit and an unwavering focus on our customer's success, we deploy best-in-class technology that solves some of the nation's greatest defense challenges'- he knew he had found a place where his experiences and values could truly make an impact.

Having personally experienced the life-saving capabilities of similar technology, Tom feels a deep connection to Numerica's work. He even expressed gratitude during his job interview, appreciating the impact of the company's contributions to national defense and his personal safety. "Even during my interview, I took the time to thank everyone for the work they do. The technology we develop here is incredibly meaningful to me."

Why do I tell you this story? My parents started Numerica Corporation in 1996.[20] The company began in humble circumstances, with a small team dedicated to solving complex problems in missile defense, as well as air and space surveillance. Founded with a boundary-pushing *'what's possible'* vision, Numerica became a significant player in national defense technology thanks to its commitment to innovation and excellence.

Tom's experience in Iraq and subsequent work at Numerica perfectly illustrate the company's mission. I met Tom shortly after he began working at Numerica, and he shared with me why he joined the team. "Every day, when I come to work, I think about how our systems can save lives, just like similar technology did for me. It serves as a powerful motivator and a continual reminder of the significance of our mission."

Tom's work at Numerica is driven by a deeper purpose. As he puts it, "It's about knowing that what we can do here can save lives and approaching every task with that in mind. How we achieve our goals is truly what defines us." For Tom, the mission isn't just about the end product—it's about the responsibility, care, and intention that he and his team bring to every step of the process. Their focus on saving lives through their technology is a testament to their personal connection to the mission. The How>What philosophy they follow emphasizes that the true impact lies not just in the results but in the dedication and approach that bring the mission to life.

Tom's story demonstrates how living out a mission with the right approach can create a lasting impact not just in the products delivered but in the lives those products protect.

THE SECRET TO A KILLER MISSION STATEMENT: KEEP IT REAL, KEEP IT CLEAR

By crafting your vision and mission from the foundation of your identity, purpose, meaning, and calling, you ensure that these guiding statements authentically represent who you or your organization are. This intentional process shapes the path you will follow, aligning every action and decision with the essence of your being. Through this alignment, your vision and mission become powerful tools that drive purposeful action, clearly focusing your aspirations and guiding you toward your desired future.

One of my favorite roles at The Coca-Cola Company was in a group called Franchise Leadership. But I was always puzzled by leaders in the Company who couldn't describe what Franchise Leadership did, let alone people inside the group. When someone on the team was asked what they do or how they contribute to the company's success, they'd have different answers, or they'd stutter and stammer. This didn't create much confidence among the executives.

I developed a concise elevator speech that helped executives understand the "mysterious" role and its value to the Company: "We inspire execution excellence and strategically align with our bottling partners by collaborating closely and fostering strong partnerships to ensure the Coca-Cola System wins in the marketplace." The idea was simple: The Company and its bottling partners were *independent companies*, but no one could stop them if they were aligned and marching to the same drum. Winning meant achieving share, revenue, and profit targets for everyone.

When I shared the mission statement with team members, executives, and bottling partners, they got it. Once they *got* it, they could *do* it. Mission statements don't need to be complicated or lengthy; they should be concise and clear. I recommend the following fill-in-the-blank formula:

We [action/what you do] by [method/how you do it] to [purpose/why you do it].

For example, *we strategically align with our bottling partners and inspire execution excellence* [action/what you do] *by collaborating closely and fostering strong partnerships* [method/how you do it] *to ensure the Coca-Cola System wins in the marketplac*e [purpose/why you do it].

Or, adapting my team's original vision statement to reflect the mission, I'd write it this way:

We positively influence our company's future [action/what you do] *by molding world-class commercial strategies, enabling exceptional execution, building authentic teams, nurturing future leaders, and celebrating our achievements* [method/how you do it] *to win the hearts of your teammates, customers, and consumers* [purpose/why you do it].

Think about it. Your mission defines what you do and the result. If you accomplish your mission, your vision will come to life. But remember, it's not just about having a mission; it's about how you make that mission a reality every day. Whether you lead a company, a team, or a group of volunteers, do you have a clear mission statement? And more importantly, do you use it to guide your everyday decisions and communications?

VISION AND MISSION: BRINGING THEM TO LIFE

Vision is what you want to be when you grow up—a mental picture of your desired future. It's the ultimate destination, the place you're aiming to reach. On the other hand, mission is what you *do* to bring that vision to life. It's the day-to-day actions, decisions, and commitments that move you closer to that future reality. And the mission is not only about the concrete steps you take to achieve the vision but also about the values, principles, and methods that guide your steps.

As a wise king wrote thousands of years ago, "For a dream comes through much activity, and a fool's voice is known by his many words." (Ecclesiastes 5:3 NKJV) With apologies to Solomon, my paraphrase would be, "A vision with no action is as worthless as words from a fool."

In my experience, having spoken and led training in hundreds of locations around the world, I often see vision and mission statements proudly displayed on posters. Yet, when I ask people to recite those statements, almost no one can do it accurately. That's because, for many, these statements are just paper tigers—words on a wall that don't resonate or inspire.

Here's the deal. Vision and mission statements need to be more than just words; they need to come alive in the hearts and minds of the people within the organization. How you live them out is what truly makes the difference. It's the way these statements are embodied in everyday actions, the way they influence decisions, and the way they shape the culture of a team or organization that brings them to life.

Without the "how," a vision remains a wish, and a mission becomes just another task. But when people understand and commit to living the vision and mission in their daily work, these statements become powerful tools for transformation. They guide behavior, unify efforts, and ultimately, lead to the fulfillment of that mental picture of the future.

STAY THE COURSE: NAVIGATING DISTRACTIONS, DOUBTERS, AND DOUBTS[21]

Ben Hunt-Davis, an Olympic contender in rowing, and his team knew that to achieve their ultimate goal, they had to be relentless in their focus. They'd failed twice in their quest for gold. Something had to change. They had to think differently. They resolved to focus on improving performance and chose to believe the results would take care of themselves.

Their guiding question became, *Will it make the boat go faster?* This single-minded approach helped them filter out anything that didn't directly contribute to their success. Let's explore how this mindset can help navigate these common vision and mission derailers:

Other Opportunities. Like Ben and his team, you'll encounter numerous opportunities that may seem attractive but don't align with your vision and mission. They were often presented with chances to engage in activities or events that, while prestigious, didn't help them achieve their goal. Would attending an event make the boat go faster? No. Decision made. For us, the *how* means assessing every opportunity with the same clarity.

Criticism. Every ambitious vision and mission attracts criticism. Ben's team faced plenty of doubters, including those close to them who didn't want to see them risk failure again. The key was how they responded—they filtered out the noise and only engaged with feedback that would help them improve. This meant acknowledging constructive criticism that could make the boat go faster while disregarding the negativity that served no purpose. For us, the how involves distinguishing between criticism that refines our vision and mission and that which drags us down.

Fear. The fear of failure was a constant companion for Ben and his team, especially after previous Olympic disappointments. However, instead of allowing fear to paralyze them, they used it as a motivator. They embraced the risks, knowing that success required stepping into the unknown. The *how* here is crucial—it's about harnessing fear as a driving force for progress rather than letting it derail our vision and mission.

Misalignment. A team can have a shared goal, but success is elusive if they aren't aligned in their approach. Ben's team learned it wasn't just about individual efforts but about rowing in unison, literally and figuratively. They synchronized their actions and mindset, ensuring every team member was committed to the same strategy. In our work, the *how* is about fostering alignment within the team, making sure everyone is not only aware of the vision and mission but also working cohesively to achieve it

At the heart of these challenges is the need for a clear, unwavering vision and mission, just as Ben Hunt-Davis and his team had. They transformed their vision into reality by staying focused on the mission. Did their dedication to the mission make the boat go faster? Indeed. They took home the gold medal. Their story serves as a powerful reminder that how we navigate these potential derailers ultimately leads to success.

THE TASTE OF FAILURE: WHY NEW COKE FELL FLAT

In 1985, Coca-Cola lost its true north. It rebranded itself with a sweeter 'New Coke' after years of Pepsi taunting it with the Pepsi Challenge, a landmark series of blind taste tests. In the ads, a parade of consumers tried Coke and Pepsi, except they didn't know which was which. The blind test would reveal to cola drinkers that they liked Pepsi over Coke. Over the ensuing years, that campaign took root in Coke's executives. They started to believe that Pepsi wasn't just beating Coke in blind taste tests but that Pepsi was becoming the cola of America.

So, Coke wasn't willing to sit back and let Pepsi rule the world. Coke struck back. On April 23, 1985, it announced New Coke. I was a high school senior. Having grown up on Coke, I would never drink Pepsi. When I heard about the switch, I bought all the 'old' Coke I could find. But when it ran out, I switched to RC Cola – anything but Pepsi.

Coca-Cola failed to understand or communicate the "how," the deeper reason people loved the brand, which led to a backlash despite all the market research and testing that said New Coke would win. Why? Coke focused on what it had to do – beat Pepsi in a head-to-head taste test – rather than how to do it, maintaining its vision of tradition and the joy that Coca-Cola brought into people's lives. They lost sight of the values that had made Coke a cultural icon. Coke wasn't a product. It was Americana and a shared sense of happiness. The brand loyalty that was decades in the making wasn't about sweetness. It was about the distinctive taste that people had learned to love.

By trying to compete with Pepsi on taste alone, Coke lost its way, forgetting how it had built such deep connections with its customers. They thought a new product would solve the problem, but they didn't realize the how—their loyalty, legacy, and unique brand experience—was far more powerful than the what of a sweeter formula.

And 79 days later, on July 11, 1985, Coca-Cola Classic returned to the market. I was one of the first in line to buy a 20-oz bottle and to toast the return of a bit of my childhood.

The moral of the story? Even the best-laid strategies will fail if they are disconnected from the vision and mission that inform them. Coke lost its way because it veered from how it was doing things, keeping its great product true to its core values – to what it was doing, changing its product.

What they got was a market so thirsty for a simple moment of joy that, by 2005, The Coca-Cola Company was back on course with the launch of Coke Zero. This time, the Company followed its original vision for delivering simple moments of joy but adapted it to suit today's consumer desires. It gave consumers the true original Coke experience but without the calories. I was personally involved in the launch of Coke Zero, and it remains my favorite soft drink to this day. The promise of great taste without the calories resonates with me—it delivers and then some. This wasn't just another product release; it was a statement of alignment with Coca-Cola's core values and mission while embracing innovation that met the evolving demands of consumers.

The fact that Coke Zero has been such a hit suggests the value of innovation in keeping your eye on the ball – the vision and mission, that is – to be true to yourself as you address the needs of the moment. 'However beautiful the strategy, you should occasionally look at the results,' Winston Churchill said. That's as true of vision and mission as it is of strategy. No matter how beautiful, lofty, or ambitious, they don't mean a thing unless they generate the results you want. Great leaders want to ensure that the visions and missions we craft are not merely aspirational but also actionable and measurable. The results are the feedback loop. They tell you whether you're on track or not.

The story of New Coke versus Coke Zero illustrates this perfectly. New Coke had a vision and mission, but it lacked alignment with the Company's true identity, leading to failure. In contrast, Coke Zero succeeded because it stayed true to the Company's core vision and mission while adapting to meet new consumer expectations.

This is where the How>What philosophy comes into play. Achieving results (the what) is important, but how you approach and execute your vision and mission makes all the difference. Coca-Cola's journey from New Coke to Coke Zero shows that when your approach aligns with your core vision and mission, you achieve not only success but also significance. You create products that resonate deeply with consumers and stand the test of time.

SUCCESS THAT ENDURES

What's the real point of all this vision and mission stuff, anyway? "Success" would be a common answer, and it's not wrong. Success, accomplishment, and checking off milestones—are all crucial. But there's more.

Several years ago, I had a transformative experience that reshaped my understanding of success. On a mission trip to the Tijuana City Dump, I met Juan, a "pepenador," a scavenger. He made his living by rummaging through trash and reselling what he recovered to local merchants. Everything that he owned came from the dump, including his clothes and his food. One man's trash is another man's treasure.

Juan and two hundred families who lived in the landfill were among the poorest of the poor in Tijuana. Homes were created with tarps, pallets, tin scraps, and old garage doors – whatever residents could find and use to build a roof over their heads. The rancid odor that rose in the summer's heat overwhelmed me, but was barely noticeable to the dump's residents.

Why was I in the dump? I volunteered to go on a mission trip with my church to serve the people who lived in the landfill. We aimed to help those who couldn't help themselves, to shed light in a dark place, and to invest our time in bringing hope to the hopeless.

Once we arrived at the dump, we spread out across the canyon, knocking on doors, giving them a gift of rice & beans, and inviting them to a Vacation Bible School. We shared that the school would include games, music, and food. We also mentioned that we'd be providing personal hygiene supplies and services at the event. Why? As you might imagine, water was a scarce resource in the dump. Showering, washing hair, and brushing teeth were all considered a luxury. But their deep need provided an opportunity to show love in action.

After making the rounds and inviting people to join us, we set up the school location, including a long series of hair-washing stations. Each station included a chair, buckets of water, and shampoo.

The only thing missing was volunteers to wash people's hair.

A mission trip leader asked, "Who'd like to wash hair today?"

Okay, I have to admit, this is where I got a little uncomfortable, put my head down and stepped back, not wanting to make eye contact with the leader.

The leader explained that women volunteers would wash women's hair, and men would wash men's. I grew a little more uncomfortable but remembered that the best way to grow is to move out of one's comfort zone and into the awkward zone.

I raised my hand and said, "I'll do it."

Soon after, the Vacation Bible School started. I was amazed at the large number of adults and children who came. We connected with people through translators, sang songs, watched skits, and shared a meal together. Considering their living conditions, I found the residents of the dump to be a kind, warm-hearted, and gracious bunch.

Then came the hair washing. Ladies first. A long line developed, and the pampering began. Next, the men lined up, and it was my turn to step up. I went to my assigned station and saw a middle-aged man being urged by his significant other to have his hair washed. He was hesitant at first, but slowly shuffled in my direction. I smiled and introduced myself to Juan as he took a seat in the chair. He didn't look me in the eye. I could tell this was a very humbling experience for him.

I slowly poured water on his head, applied shampoo, and washed his lice-infested, thick, black hair. It only took a few minutes, and when we were finished, Juan offered the most valuable and heartfelt gratuity he could - a bright smile and "gracias" as he looked me in the eye, man to man. He waved goodbye and left with his family.

I may never see Juan again or know how his life turned out. I do know that he experienced a moment of happiness and refreshment, and that I played a small role in it. The experience was huge for me. It was the genesis of my shift from a success mindset to a significance mindset.

Success is about hitting targets and achieving measurable goals, while significance goes beyond that to create a *lasting* impact. It's not just what we accomplish but how we achieve those outcomes that leave the world a little better than we found it.

When we set our sights on a vision and mission, we often fixate on the end goal. But it's the way we breathe life into that vision and mission—the how—that separates a successful endeavor from one of true significance. The significance mindset dares us to look for the deeper purpose and legacy of our actions.

While outcomes are important, they are just the starting point. True significance emerges from the way we achieve those results—how we lead, interact with others, and remain true to our values and purpose.

As you ponder your leadership journey, consider this: Is your vision and mission inspiring others to succeed *and* create a lasting significance?

It's the difference between merely meeting an objective and leaving the world better than we found it—if only for a moment.

By aligning your actions with who you are and your why, you transform vision into reality—a reality that improves people's lives. In the process, important "stuff" gets done.

Vision is crucial, but it's meaningless without measurement in human terms.

PRINCIPLE

Act with Vision

QUESTIONS

How clearly have you articulated the future you want to create for your organization or team? Does your vision inspire others to see themselves as part of that future, and do they understand how their daily work contributes to it?

_____
_____
_____

What specific actions and decisions are you taking to bring your vision to life? How does your mission guide the way you and your team approach each task, ensuring alignment with your long-term goals?

_____
_____
_____

Are you and your team focused solely on achieving success, or are you also considering the lasting impact of your actions? How can you shift your mindset from merely hitting targets to creating a meaningful and enduring legacy?

_____
_____
_____

CHAPTER 4

Talk Is Cheap

> "The single biggest problem in communication
> is the illusion that it has taken place."
> — GEORGE BERNARD SHAW

The five-hour flight began with a festive atmosphere. Cocktails were flowing, and conversations quickly moved from professional to personal. "Get ready to hand out the visas," the executive directed. The company plane and its C-suite passengers were en route to Bogotá, Colombia, for a brief market visit.

To enter Colombia, each passenger needed a visa along with their passport. The executive delegated the visa application process to an assistant and requested that the permits be available for distribution just before arriving in Bogotá.

Upon final approach, the executive gave the assistant the go-ahead to distribute the visas. He proudly produced a packet and began handing out the small envelopes. But something was wrong.

I'll bet you already guessed. The assistant purchased Visa *gift cards* instead of the required travel visas. No documents meant no entry into Colombia. "How could you possibly screw this up?!"

"I thought this was a pleasure trip, and you wanted gift cards to cover expenses," the assistant replied. "You said nothing about travel visas."

The plane had to turn around and go back home.

Can you imagine the embarrassment and frustration? So much wasted time. An expensive case study in broken communication. But who's to blame?

The executive? Yes. She assumed that the directive was clear and understood.

The assistant? Yes. He assumed what was meant by the directive and acted erroneously.

This story highlights the importance of not just talking but truly *connecting* to ensure understanding.

BEYOND WORDS: THE TRUE ESSENCE OF COMMUNICATION

We are bombarded by 10,000 ads per day.[22] We speak about 16,000 words per day[23] and hear up to 30,000 words per day.[24] Talk is cheap.

All well and good. But studies show that we only absorb about 25% of what we hear.[25] Don't believe me? Without looking at the paragraph above, do you remember how many ads we're shown every day?

Couple that with the fact that a third of all teenagers are on one of five main social media platforms almost constantly. Studies show that they're losing the ability to interpret body language, facial expressions, vocal tone and pitch, boundaries, and personal space.[26]

But that's not all. Loneliness is at an all-time high. "As the American workday becomes more faceless and scheduled, the number of U.S. adults who call themselves lonely has climbed to 58% from 46% in 2018," a Cigna poll of 10,000 Americans recently reported."[27]

The inability to *connect*, let alone communicate, can lead to dire consequences.

What's the solution to all this disconnect? Truly connecting with others.

Connection is the ability to go beyond communicating information—getting to know people, expressing empathy, building trust, and demonstrating the ability to help them. Cultivating a genuine connection goes beyond mere exchanges of information; it becomes the foundation for thriving collaborations, sparking innovation, and strengthening bonds.

Connection is the cornerstone of communication.

Talk may be cheap, but connection, expensive as it may be, is worth every penny.

BEYOND BUSINESS: HOW A THEME PARK DAY BUILT A BRIDGE

"Rob is one of the most difficult people to get to know and very hard to work with. Over the past twenty years, few company representatives successfully developed a relationship with him, let alone were able to influence him. He can be very disagreeable and non-inclusive."

This is what my peers told me as I took my new role working with our partner company's new Senior Vice President, Rob. I had the demanding task of building trust with him and becoming a valued member of his team. Early in my new role, I was invited to a meeting at Universal Studios in Orlando. I reviewed the invitation list and saw that Rob was attending the meeting. What a perfect opportunity to get to know him.

As I arrived in Orlando, I received an email stating that the team would be gathering in the hotel lobby at 3 pm and would be heading to the amusement park together. I arrived in the lobby along with thirty other meeting attendees. Everyone was there except Rob. I asked where he was, and they said he was running late.

We decided to wait a few minutes, but most of the group became restless, and folks slowly left a few at a time. I asked some of the team members before they went if they wanted to wait on Rob, and they said, "No, we want to have fun at the park. We'll catch up with him later." I considered going with them, but decided to stick it out and wait for him.

About fifteen minutes later, Rob came running into the lobby. The small group that remained greeted him after he checked in. He told us that he wanted to go to the park and asked where everyone else was. We told him that the group had gone ahead to the park and that we could catch up with them. He nodded his head in disappointment.

Then, he pulled out a map of the amusement park. Rob enthusiastically showed us how he'd mapped out all of the rides he wanted to take, including Harry Potter, Spider-Man, and the Dueling Dragons roller coaster. He confessed his love for amusement parks and said he'd been looking forward to the team-building afternoon in the park for quite a while. I exclaimed, "What are we waiting for? Let's go!"

Because the group was small, I had the chance to hang out with Rob in the park all afternoon. Waiting in lines and enjoying the rides together, I got to know him. We talked about families, hobbies, travel, current events, and even a little business on the side. Rob warmed to me and appreciated the small group going to the park with him.

Over time, I earned Rob's trust. He began including me in meetings, and anytime I emailed Rob with a question or sought his help, he'd email me right back. He always picked up the phone whenever I called. Why? I attribute it to intentionally connecting with him at the park.

This story exemplifies the How > What philosophy: It wasn't just about the team-building event at the amusement park (the what) but about how I approached the opportunity to connect with Rob with genuine interest and patience.

Never miss an opportunity to connect with others—that's the "ride" you really want to take.

GRACE IN THE GRIND: HOW DIGNITY CAN CHANGE A CAREER PATH

"Don't hire Steve. He's not a good fit. If you do, it will be a mistake." I heard this from a few key leaders after seeking their advice.

"He has the right experience and transferable skills. . ... With a little coaching, he'll be great. . .." This is what a trusted peer who highly recommended Steve told me.

With polar opposite recommendations and little time to decide, the pressure was on to hire an associate to work with our business partners. I needed to recruit, interview, and fill the position within two weeks, or I'd lose the headcount. If I lost the headcount, the work and relationship management would fall on my plate.

I moved swiftly and chose to hire Steve. Why? I saw potential, or so I told myself. I heard what I wanted to hear from the positive advice and ignored the others. I believed that I could single-handedly develop Steve's analytical, relationship-building, and leadership skills. This wasn't confidence, it was arrogance.

Fast forward one year. Developing Steve required a significant amount of time and energy. Even though I had ten other team members and was accountable for eighteen markets, I spent 80 percent of my time with him and his specific market.

I didn't want Steve to fail. I saw his success as my responsibility, having decided against the counsel of others. I wanted to prove that I could help him reach his potential. Over time, his business partners rejected him because of a perceived lack of credibility. Steve was no longer invited to meetings or trade rides, and as a result, he lost his ability to influence or add value. I shared the feedback from the business partners with Steve along the way. We developed a plan to enhance his performance and strengthen his connection with the business partner. But Steve didn't follow through on the plan. I finally came to the realization that I couldn't develop Steve as I thought. His skill set and motivational fit weren't right for the role.

I made a mistake. A change was needed for Steve's benefit, for my team, for our company, for our business partners, and for me.

Now, I had another decision to make. Should I place Steve on a formal Performance Improvement Plan (PIP) to potentially terminate his employment with the company? After consulting with my leadership and human resources, we elected to place Steve on a PIP. It was a tough decision, but the right one.

Then, I prayed for Steve. I prayed that he'd be able to improve his performance or that God would provide for him if the PIP didn't conclude with positive results. I also prayed for wisdom and a sensitive heart as I revealed the tough news to him.

I reached out to Steve to share our decision. As you can imagine, he wasn't happy. Steve said, "*No one* else faced the challenging environment and partners like I have." He demanded that I delay the PIP.

I wouldn't. We'd put plans in place before, but he hadn't acted on them. I listed several other performance-related issues and said no.

Frustrated, he blurted, "I was doing my job well—I just didn't get along with people." Then he paused for a moment as he realized the irony. "I feel like such a failure."

I was moved by Steve's emotions. I'd come to like Steve very much and wanted to encourage him.

"Speaking from my heart, you are still valued and need to separate what is happening from who you are. It is up to you to improve. Ninety percent don't make it through the process, but the ten percent experience a wonderful career transformation."

A few weeks passed, and Steve didn't make it through the PIP process and was about to be let go. Then, something unexpected happened. A role opened up in another part of the company that better suited his skill set and was the perfect motivational fit. (Steve had been under the microscope so long that we had a clear idea of his strengths and weaknesses.) Typically, an associate wasn't eligible to interview for other roles while under a PIP. Because of what seemed like a perfect job fit, my HR partner and I extended grace to Steve and approved his interview. Showing Steve dignity, we agreed that sometimes people are in the wrong role, and I wanted to do the right thing for him.

And guess what? He got the job!

This experience taught me a couple of valuable lessons:

- *Be an Unselective Listener.* Although I sought wise counsel from others, I selectively listened to what they had to say. I pieced together what I wanted to hear and rationalized my decision. Admittedly, I had my own agenda, was stubborn, and acted out of arrogance. If I'd listened early on, Steve and I—and our partners—wouldn't have suffered through the challenging circumstances. When seeking counsel, listen objectively to others and refrain from filtering your thoughts with predetermined biases.
- *Show Dignity and Respect for Others.* During challenging circumstances with Steve, I always tried to encourage him, help him feel valued, and be genuine with him. I remained hopeful and professional. That's the way I'd want to be treated. Wouldn't you?

This story also illustrates the How>What philosophy: It's not just about the actions taken (the what), but *how* those actions were carried out—with care and a commitment to doing the right thing—that made a difference. Connecting with others begins with valuing them. As leaders, it's essential to pour ourselves into others, even when we may not see immediate results. By showing genuine care and respect, we can have a profoundly positive impact on others' lives. We might not know how the story will end, but treating others as truly valuable always leads to better outcomes.

WALK A MILE IN THEIR SHOES-BEFORE OPENING YOUR MOUTH

What is empathy? Concern for the welfare of others. The ability to detect or anticipate the emotions and thoughts of others. Empathy can only happen when you highly value someone.

I'm not naturally empathetic. But it is possible to intentionally grow in this area, personally and professionally.

1. *Avoid making assumptions.* Your view of the world is limited. Others have lived a different reality. If you're from a well-off and intact family from the United States, you don't have a clue what it's like to grow up in an orphanage in Ukraine or suffer through a war. If you've never lost a job, avoid assuming that you know exactly what that experience feels like. Making assumptions only gets in the way of developing empathy.

2. *Ask questions.* One way to understand someone is to ask questions. Develop a genuine interest in them. Develop the habit of asking open-ended questions, which gives people freedom to gently dismantle your assumptions.

3. *Listen.* Listening intently is connected to asking questions and avoiding assumptions. Seek to understand the emotions and motivations of others. When you genuinely listen to them, empathy emerges.

4. *Try on someone else's shoes.* Ask yourself, *what would I be thinking and feeling if I were in this situation?* Just asking yourself this question is the most significant step you can take toward being empathetic.

5. *Be present.* Give your undivided attention to others. You can't be empathetic if you're thinking about something else while someone is speaking to you. For example, I'm trying

to finish this paragraph while my wife is telling me about a situation at her job. (*I'd better stop typing—right now.*) We're not as good at hiding our disinterest as we think.
6. *Practice having meaningful conversations.* Yes, practice. Talking about sports is fine, but it's not a personal topic unless you're talking to me about the Broncos. One way to get the ball rolling is to discuss something meaningful to you openly. Then, ask questions. The more vulnerable you are willing to share, the more you'll receive in return. Be open, and others will be more open with you.

It's not enough to understand another person's viewpoint; empathy isn't a one-way street. It's ultimately about approaching every interaction with care and humility towards another person. And when we go out of our way to do that, we engage in the practice of How>What. We shift the focus away from just what we're doing and instead seek to enhance the quality of our relationships, instill trust and respect, and fundamentally pay attention in a way that truly matters.

FROM GAS TO GIGGLES: THE POWER OF LAUGHTER AT WORK

During a Coca-Cola staff meeting, we shared what we had for lunch. Someone had yogurt, and another had a candy bar. I volunteered that I went to Burger King and had an Impossible Whopper for lunch. My manager asked, "Did you have gas?"

I paused, and then we all laughed.

I said, "I feel okay, I think . . ." Atlanta was in the middle of a gasoline shortage, and my manager wondered if I had enough gasoline to drive to Burger King—not about my digestive tract status.

Laughter is the shortest distance between two people. It breaks down walls and repairs relationships. A good sense of humor can smooth out awkward situations and take the edge off intense conversations. Research indicates that humor fosters team cohesion, alleviates stress, and enhances productivity.

Tips for Using Humor at Work
- *Stay Safe.* Be diplomatic and steer clear of sensitive topics. Silly is better than sarcastic.
- *Pace Yourself.* Use humor sparingly so it remains effective. Humor is the seasoning, not the entrée.
- *Know Your Audience.* Different companies have different cultures—adjust accordingly.

This story perfectly illustrates the How>What philosophy: It's not just about what was said (the joke), but how it was told and the shared laughter that followed. Humor and shared moments create connections that go beyond the surface level. These moments can build stronger teams, reduce stress, and foster a positive atmosphere.

BELONGING OVER BOSSINESS: HOW ONE BLUE SHIRT CHANGED THE GAME

What's the secret formula that turns a group of people into a cohesive team? The answer lies in one powerful word: Belonging. It's the magic ingredient that wraps you in comfort, filling you with confidence and a sense of connection. It's more than a warm, fuzzy feeling—it's the rocket fuel that drives employee engagement, job satisfaction, productivity, and success.

Picture this: When I first joined The Hershey Company's Sales Development team, I knew I was stepping into the big leagues—a dozen top performers and me, the new guy. I was warned to be humble and not "shine too brightly." And whatever I did, I needed to keep an eye on a fellow named Chad.

Now, Chad was your classic overachiever, with just enough arrogance to make sure everyone knew it. He took an immediate dislike to me, bragging about his plans to become president of the company and ominously warning that he'd be "watching" me.

But it was during a town hall meeting in the grand Hershey Theater that Chad's one-upmanship took a bizarre twist. As I settled into my seat, who parked himself next to me? You guessed it, Chad.

He glanced at my outfit and frowned. "You really should think more about how you dress. You're wearing a blue dress shirt, and the rest of our team is wearing white." I looked down the row, and sure enough, everyone was in white. I felt like I'd worn a party hat to a board meeting.

Embarrassment gnawed at me throughout the meeting. I couldn't shake the feeling that I'd made a "career-limiting" move. Later that day, I shared the incident with my team lead, Paul, who burst out laughing and reassured me, "Chad's just trying to intimidate you. Don't worry about it."

The next day, I walked into a meeting to find a surprise waiting for me. My teammates had decided to wear blue shirts to show their support and make me feel welcome. Chad was still in white, but the focus was on the team's gesture of unity and inclusion. I couldn't help but smile, and my teammates returned the gesture.

After the meeting, Paul explained, "We wanted to send a message. We're a team, and we stick together. We also want you to know that you belong here."

That day, a blue shirt became a symbol of acceptance. I realized that strong leaders instill a sense of belonging and help others feel secure and valued.

Here are some principles that will build a sense of belonging and transform your team:

- *The Importance of Team Unity and Support.* How can you foster unity and support in your team? By celebrating the uniqueness of each member and acknowledging and supporting their individuality, you reinforce the idea that everyone has a place.
- *The Impact of Intimidation Tactics.* Even seemingly insignificant actions or words can have a profound impact on others, as seen in Chad's comment about my blue shirt. It underscores the need to watch out for words and actions that create a sense of unbelonging and take actions to reinforce the value of unity.
- *The Symbolism of Small Gestures.* Small symbols can carry profound meanings, as seen in the sea of blue shirts that welcomed me. What symbols or gestures could strengthen your team's bond? Create shared symbols that reflect your team's values and connection.

Everyone has a role to play; each voice matters, and true belonging is not about blending in but about standing out—together.

COLD WAR OR WARM WELCOME? HOW DIPLOMACY DEFUSES TENSION

I learned how critical grace and understanding are for conversations and conflict firsthand through the workshop I facilitated in Moscow, Russia. In 2019, I was invited to Moscow to facilitate a Partnering for Growth (P4G) workshop between The Coca-Cola Company and one of its bottlers, Coca-Cola Hellenic Bottling Company, to help them form a strategic business partnership. During the two-day workshop, the teams and their new leaders worked to assimilate around a new vision of the partnership, exploring shared values, learning about each other's operating models (including financial metrics and key business drivers), clarifying roles and responsibilities, and drafting common capability plans.

After the first day, I joined the two leadership teams for dinner. We ordered our first round of beverages, and then it got quiet. I asked the team what was on their mind, and they wanted to know if I was open to answering some questions about America's political landscape. I didn't want to offend them, so I said, "Why not?"

They asked me who I voted for in the 2016 presidential election and why. I tactfully revealed my vote and explained my rationale. Then, I wondered if *they* were open to some questions. In their excellent English, they echoed with a smile and a "Why not?"

I asked the group what they thought of former President Ronald Reagan. The room grew quiet. Then someone disparaged Reagan and said he was a "tired old man who loved his wife." I was stunned. *The leader of the free world. How dare you?* Rather than becoming defensive, I became curious and shifted the conversation by asking them about Mikhail Gorbachev, the former Russian leader. They passionately explained that he sold Russia out and compromised too much. They recounted stories of waiting in breadlines for food; their childhoods were marked by poverty and scarcity. From their perspective, Russia was left in shambles after the USSR fell. Lastly, the group shared that they loved Vladimir Putin because of the country's status and prosperity. I could sense their disdain for America and zeal for their motherland, Russia.

Later in the evening, I offered a toast to the group, thanking them for participating in the workshop and inspiring them to do great things together. I shared a quote by Mother Theresa, "You can do what I cannot do. I can do what you cannot do. Together, we can do great things." Then, an inebriated co-worker and Russian expat yelled, "You're such a f***ing American." "What do you mean?" I replied. She continued, "That was very western of you!" Some laughed. Some cringed. Thoroughly embarrassed, I forced a smile, took a big swig of wine, and shrank in my seat. *Didn't see that one coming.* Friendly fire.

The good news is that I was able to maintain my composure. Before my trip, I studied their culture and learned that Russians prefer to build relationships first and then focus on completing tasks afterward. Trust—then collaborate. If I expressed any animosity, I would have self-sabotaged the P4G workshop even before it started.

The next morning, a couple of Russian workshop participants pulled me aside and apologized for the conversation at dinner. I reassured them that I wasn't offended at all and explained that it's essential for people to talk, connect, and understand each other's perspectives. We don't do it enough in America; we are so polarized, and as a result, nothing gets done. This leads to a lot of resentment, anger, and what I call a "Civil Cold War."

With that, the rest of the workshop proceeded smoothly. The participants were transparent about their business relationship and shared their concerns. After airing their opinions, the participants were eager to resolve differences, create common goals, and build a sense of community. They developed improvement action plans, assigned responsibilities, and scheduled routine follow-up meetings to ensure progress. At the end of the workshop, leaders from both entities presented me with a participant-signed Coca-Cola/FIFA 2018 Russia World Cup soccer ball. Something I treasure to this day.

But it all started with that dinner conversation I'll never forget. It was a test, really. I was in a foreign land, representing not only my company but also my country, and I needed to be a diplomat. Had I lost my composure, I never would have connected with the team and failed in my mission to bring them together. After all, diplomacy is supposed to nurture positive connections. Here's a six-pack of principles I learned about diplomacy:

- *Think before you speak.* A wise man once told me, "Just because you think something doesn't mean you need to say it." I've learned to listen first, then take what I heard, let it sink in, and decide how to respond. Sometimes, the best response is no response—like keeping the toothpaste in the tube; some thoughts are better left unsaid.
- *Choose your words carefully.* To respond, play chess in your head, thinking two or three moves ahead. Consider the consequences of what you're going to say and where you want to end up. The Chinese philosopher Lao-Tzu said, "Respond intelligently, even to unintelligent treatment." By anticipating outcomes, you can prepare a response.
- *Stay cool.* Surprises will occur, and you'll need to stay calm. Identify your hot buttons—what triggers your anger, prickliness, or impatience. Instead of responding with hostility, adopt a considerate and graceful approach. Lead by being a calming influence amid conflict or crisis, whether by taking deep breaths, pausing before speaking, or practicing active listening.
- *Be aware of non-verbal communication.* Psychologists tell us that 93% of communication is about body language and tone of voice, with only 7% being words. People can read you like a book. They will interpret your eyes, tone, body language, and 'vibe.' It's not about what you're saying, but how you say it, that's often more effective. A smile or a softened tone can make a difference.
- *Recognize and appreciate diversity of thought.* Everyone has an opinion, and as a leader, it's crucial to understand what people think and why. Ask probing questions and listen intently without taking offense. Seek common ground—you never know what you might learn. By exploring my peers'

thoughts on past leaders, I discovered different perspectives on the story that I hadn't considered.
- *Focus on relationships.* In many cultures, including Russia, building relationships comes before accomplishing tasks. Establish trust and win hearts before asking for their hand. Building rapport and trust through informal interactions is essential for long-term success. My experience in Russia taught me that trust forms the foundation for effective collaboration. And trust can be earned in unexpected or uncomfortable ways.

This story underscores the How>What philosophy: It's not just about having a conversation (the what), but how you engage in that conversation—with empathy, curiosity, and respect—that makes a difference. The principles of diplomacy I've shared aren't just tactics for international workshops; they're essential tools for any leader aiming to foster trust and collaboration.

Diplomacy is saying what you want to say (honesty) but resisting all the wrong impulses on how to say it.

Choose the right "how" and the Cold War will thaw.

PRINCIPLE
Connect beyond words

QUESTIONS

Look at your calendar for tomorrow or next week. When is your next one-on-one meeting? It's time to practice! Instead of preparing for the conversation by only focusing on the business at hand, take three minutes to consider the person you're meeting with. What might it be like to be in their shoes? (Especially as it relates to the conversation)

_____
_____
_____

On a scale of 1 - 10, how much might they have a sense of belonging on the team?

_____
_____
_____

How much do you know about them on a personal level? Prepare two appropriate questions.

_____
_____
_____

What challenges are present, and *how* can you diplomatically address them?

_____
_____
_____

What challenges have *you* been dealing with, and how might you share them in a personal way that shows humility and honesty?

_____

_____

_____

CHAPTER 5

Stop Building Trust

"Always do right.
This will gratify some people and astonish the rest."
– MARK TWAIN

Do you remember *Top Gun: Maverick*'s climactic scene? As Maverick flew away from enemy territory, his F-14 clipped the roof of a building and lost its front landing gear. With the odds stacked against him, Maverick and his co-pilot, Rooster, engaged in an epic dogfight with two enemy jets. After some heart-stopping maneuvers, Maverick and Rooster managed to take out one of the jets, but the other one seemed to be chasing him down with no escape in sight. Maverick knew this was his last mission. Suddenly, a miracle happened. A Top Gun pilot came out of nowhere, destroyed the enemy, and rescued Maverick, Rooster, and his plane. As the aircraft steadied after the enemy's relentless pursuit, Maverick asked, "Who was that?" The other pilot replied with a grin, "Your savior!"

This movie scene is analogous to my experience over the last few weeks at my former company. After 21.5 years of service, I felt like I had lost my landing gear and was being pursued by an enemy. When all seemed hopeless, my savior saved the day, and I came in for a crash landing.

An Unforeseen Accusation

It all began on a Monday morning, May 23, 2022. I'd just emailed my official retirement notice to my manager, informing him that my last day would be June 30—a moment I'd been anticipating for years. In a few weeks, on June 26, I'd turn 55 and be eligible to walk away on my terms with full benefits, just what I'd worked so hard for. I was on cloud nine.

But my mood changed in an instant.

Later that afternoon, I received a meeting invite from the Corporate Audit Department for the next day. The subject line read: Confidential Discussion. I got a sick feeling and a lump in my throat. What could this be about, I wondered.

As the virtual meeting unfolded the next day, May 24, two ethics compliance investigators revealed that I had been accused of a grave violation of the Business Code of Conduct. "You're the subject of a Business Code of Conduct investigation," said the lead ethics investigator.

A shiver of dread ran down my spine at the potential consequences of such an accusation.

According to an anonymous source, the lead investigator claimed I was non-compliant on two fronts. First, I previously conducted a leadership workshop for company employees in Las Vegas and took advantage of the opportunity by charging my company for it. Second, I was using previously conducted workshops to promote my personal platform.

Planning for the Second Half

You may be wondering how I got to this point. How about a bit of background?

In 2015, I read Bob Buford's book *Halftime* and became aware of the *Sigmoid Curve* and the importance of planning for the second half of life after the apex of one's career. Many people retire without a plan, and instead of thriving in retirement, they often fall into misery and failure. I was determined to experience the opposite. In fact, by applying the principles in this book, I clarified my identity, purpose, sense of meaning, calling, vision, and mission to create significance in retirement. I produced content and built a platform before leaving my company, with the intention of transitioning into a speaking, training, and executive coaching practice immediately after retirement. I completed this task independently, utilizing my resources.

I obtained my John Maxwell Team Certification in 2016, which granted me access to leadership and communication content that I used to build my platform. I also designed a website detailing my speaking, training, and executive coaching services, as well as their associated fees for external opportunities, all of which are intended to be rendered during personal time.

In 2018, I transitioned into a capabilities role with my employer, where I designed and delivered training to 500 internal associates. A peer familiar with my John Maxwell certification asked if I'd be open to facilitating some leadership training for one of the company's most significant partners. After receiving approval from my manager and the ethics office, and with travel expense support, I agreed. I conducted three leadership workshops for a significant partner in various cities, catering to 150 mid-level managers. In 2019, my efforts were rewarded with an invitation to lead multiple workshops for 300 mid-level managers. It was an excellent opportunity to leverage my John Maxwell certification and provide leadership training to a significant partner. The bottom line is that my personal and professional pursuits were aligned, and the results opened up new opportunities with my employer.

Vegas Shadow

Fast forward to 2022. Following the COVID-19 pandemic, I was once again asked to conduct multiple leadership workshops as an extension of my capabilities role. The first request was an internal one, to deliver a session for around 25 of my colleagues in Las Vegas.

I'd never been to Las Vegas, but I had an inexplicable gut feeling that something wasn't right.

On April 13, I led a workshop called "The Power of Influence." It was a highly interactive session that explored the concepts of influence and connection with others. Before the workshop, I had a conversation with a few longtime colleagues and revealed to them that I was planning to retire by the end of June. I departed Las Vegas the day after, feeling fulfilled because I had the opportunity to assist a group of my peers. Everything was going according to plan.

But what happens in Vegas doesn't stay in Vegas; it stays with you like a dark shadow.

Conflict of Interest

"You're the subject of a Business Code of Conduct investigation," said the lead ethics investigator.

I never imagined I'd ever hear those words. The experience was surreal and terrifying—not because I thought I'd done something wrong, but because of the sheer magnitude of the accusations.

He continued, "the allegation stems from the recent workshop you conducted in Las Vegas. Someone complained that you've violated the Code's Conflict of Interest clause. The complaint inquired about how you were able to charge the company for the workshop and benefit financially."

The Company's Business Code of Conduct aims to protect its brands and defines integrity standards. It's meant to help associates act honestly and ethically, uphold the Company's values, and protect its reputation. Employees, including me, participated in annual training, verified that they understood the Code, and were expected to comply. Violations can result in compensation penalties or *termination* of employment.

My heart sank, especially as I was on the verge of retirement—a retirement that hinged on the benefits I'd earned.

A conflict arises when personal interests interfere with an employee's business decisions, such as outside speeches or presentations. The Code reads, "If the content discusses matters related to the company, approval may also be required from the manager, Public Affairs, Legal Counsel, and others. Conflict occurs if offered payment or reimbursement in connection with making a presentation."

I was perplexed when I heard that someone had accused me of gaining financial benefit from the workshop. After all, I had only included speaking, training, and executive coaching fees on my website, along with the workshop topics and dates, although not the audience. The accuser had taken it upon themselves to deduce that I had charged the company for my services.

Moreover, the timing of the complaint was highly suspicious, as it was filed immediately after I announced my retirement. It left me wondering why someone had gone through the trouble of filing a complaint against me.

Anxiety and Uncertainty

To be crystal clear, the allegation was false.

I did not benefit financially from the Company for the Las Vegas event or any other workshop I conducted beginning in 2018. If I had benefited, there would have been a master service agreement, a statement of work, management approval, a purchase order, an invoice, and a payment. In other words, a paper trail. None of these existed in any form or fashion, nor did the intent to benefit financially.

The investigator began inquiring about my writing, speaking, and publishing activities, as well as my involvement in my family's company and my activities outside of work. I'll be the first to raise my hand and admit I'm imperfect. But the investigator's questions were an invasion of privacy, had nothing to do with my job, and found no conflict of interest. Additionally, I'd gone above and beyond to always disclose my activities, ensuring there was no appearance of a conflict of interest.

The investigator concluded the conversation by asking me to send some follow-up information to him and saying that our discussion was highly confidential. A gag order was issued—I wasn't allowed to speak to anyone, not even my manager, about the allegation. The investigation was ongoing and would include additional interviews. Lastly, he informed me that the Business Code of Conduct Infractions Committee would meet on June 13 to rule on my case, which meant I would have to wait three excruciating weeks.

As I hung up, I realized the potential ramifications of the indictment. Georgia is an "At Will" state, meaning my employment could be terminated for any reason. The charge jeopardized my hard-earned retirement benefits, including health insurance and pension. And my reputation was at risk - if I were fired for wrongdoing, I'd lose all credibility, and my post-retirement plans would go down the drain.

The investigation results and final verdict were beyond my control. All I could do was pray and hope for the best possible outcome. But the anxiety I experienced was real – a tight chest, critical self-talk, and sleepless nights.

Finding Peace and Trust during Turmoil
Amid the waiting period, my wife and I went to Greece to celebrate our 30th wedding anniversary. We planned the trip long before the conflict-of-interest charge was filed against me. Our time together

was an interesting mix of romance and high anxiety. I'd vacillate between the two extremes. Let's just say it wasn't an easy time.

In addition to this, I was delighted to learn that my book, *Discipled Leader*, had won the 2022 Selah Award for Best Nonfiction Book of the Year. Because of the cloud of suspicion I was under, I couldn't fully enjoy the honor.

Toward the end of the week, after much prayer and reflection, I remember floating in the Aegean Sea and hearing a still, small voice say, "Be still and know that I am God." At that moment, I let go of my anxiety and decided to trust God with the outcome, good or not-so-good. Then I sensed that God was whispering penetrating questions like, "What happens if you are cleared? How will you react? Will you be angry and resentful? Will you let the seed of bitterness grow into seeking revenge?"

An Unforgettable Moment

We arrived home on June 10, and after a weekend of recovering from jet lag, I flew to Grand Rapids, MI, on June 13 for work, the same day the Infractions Committee met to discuss my case. The news didn't come that day or the next. I distinctly remember sitting in the Grand Rapids airport before my flight home, drinking a beer, and mustering the courage to reach out to the lead investigator. I typed an instant message inquiring about the status of my case. The investigator immediately replied, "Have you not heard from your manager yet? He's been advised of your status. Please reach out to him."

Immediately, fingers shaking, I sent my manager a note asking if he had time to talk; it was urgent! His delayed response was, "Is there something wrong?" I replied, "Do you know the status of my Business Code of Conduct case and the Infractions Committee ruling?" Another delay. I stepped into the restroom. Then my phone buzzed. I received a message notification while standing at the urinal. I looked at my phone, and my manager responded, "You've been cleared of all charges." A moment I'll never forget.

Interestingly, my manager didn't know that I knew I was under investigation. He was aware of my case status but didn't share it due to the imposed communication gap. Since there was a strict gag order, he mistakenly assumed I was unaware of it.

I was acquitted.

Thank God. Thank my Savior.

What a relief. I would retire with full benefits and an untarnished reputation.

Three Lessons Learned on Integrity, Attitude, and Victimhood

But that's not the end of this story. Before I continue, allow me to share three valuable lessons I learned from this experience:

Put Integrity to the Test. Integrity's test is a great way to examine our character and moral standards. It is okay to be tested if we are honest and uphold our values. This can be a challenge in situations where we may be tempted to lie or act unethically for personal gain. However, it is essential to remember that integrity will always be rewarded in the long run. People who remain true to themselves and their values will be respected and ultimately achieve greater success than those who choose to be dishonest. No one is perfect, but it is essential to be consistent and honest in our actions, regardless of the consequences.

Become better, not bitter. No matter what happens, we have the power to choose how we react and respond to our circumstances. We can choose to become better, not bitter. It is up to us to make the most of our situation, no matter how difficult it may be. The challenge is to be mindful of our reactions to difficult situations. It can be easy to become bitter, but choosing positivity, resilience, and personal growth is much more beneficial. It is essential to take the time to evaluate our thoughts and feelings, ensuring we make the best decisions for our well-being. It is also important to surround ourselves with positive people and environments who will help us grow from the experience.

Reject Victimhood. This was my mantra for the last few weeks of my career. I appreciated that the company was following procedure and must address all Code of Business Conduct complaints. I hold no ill will and understand that the investigators were doing their job. The challenges I faced ultimately led to positive outcomes. I experienced victory on the other side of the fiery trial, and for *all* those reasons, I am grateful.

A FINAL CHOICE TO MAKE

As I took my seat on the plane in Grand Rapids, you'd assume I felt relief wash over me, right? Far from it. Anger had me in its grip. As the plane rose, so did my frustration. *How could anyone accuse me of something I didn't do?* I was consumed by resentment and pride, fixated on seeking revenge and ensuring justice was served.

To blow off some steam a few days later (yes, I was steaming for quite a while), I rode my bike and listened to an *Insight for Living* podcast. Pastor Chuck Swindoll was teaching "Life's Most Subtle Temptation" - revenge. He shared the Bible story of David and King Saul (1 Samuel 24).

David had been unjustly pursued by Saul, who had been convinced that David was out to kill him. One day, David and his men were hiding in a cave, and Saul entered, not knowing they were there. David's followers encouraged him to kill Saul while he had the chance, but David chose a different path. He cut a corner of Saul's robe and let him go, believing revenge was God's to take.

After Saul had left, David approached him and revealed the swatch from his robe. He confronted Saul and told him he could have killed him, but chose not to. David also explained that the allegations against him were false. Saul was humbled and said, "You are a better man than I am." Then, they parted ways.

David's story reminded me to leave revenge in God's hands and to focus on living a life of integrity and truth. With the Lord's whispered questions still ringing in my ears, I faced a critical choice: bitterness and resentment or a better way forward.

On June 16, 2022, I committed to choosing joy and thanked the Lord for His help in guiding me in the right direction. I wrote in my journal, "I felt worn out, roughed up, hungover, frustrated, and angry. Pissed that I was treated this way. Under investigation right before I leave. Was hoping to leave without a bitter taste in my mouth. I need to choose joy and be thankful. No resentment. Lord, please help me work through this and fill me with your Spirit. May my thoughts and actions honor you."

With retirement right around the corner, I recommitted to the outlook on life that had sustained me before. With the Lord's help, I ditched the weight of resentment and took flight, soaring like Maverick with friends cheering me on. I let go of the past and embraced the future, determined to make the most of my life.

This journey of facing false accusations and navigating an intense investigation process exemplifies the How>What philosophy by highlighting the critical role of integrity and resilience in leadership. While the "what" involved dealing with an unfounded accusation and the subsequent investigation, the "how" showcases an unwavering commitment to maintaining integrity, trusting in faith, and choosing to reject bitterness.

Did I handle the unexpected attack perfectly? Nope. The pressure it brought revealed some "cracks." Simply put, I was an emotional wreck. At least I didn't damage my company relationships in the process. It was also an opportunity to assess and grow.

True leadership lies in how challenges are handled with integrity and grace—perfection comes gradually. Remember, it's not just about what you do but how you do it that defines your legacy as a leader. How you carry yourself and how you treat others are the building blocks of trust.

INTEGRITY: NOT JUST A BUZZWORD

What do you think of when you read the word "integrity?" Do you roll your eyes and think, *Oh no, here we go again? What a tired, old topic? Just go away!*

But you've got to ask yourself, *why do we keep bumping into it?* Just look at some recent headlines screaming about the lack of integrity:

"Two Former Presidents of Boilermakers International Union Among Seven Indicted for $20M Embezzlement Scheme."[28]

"Former Alabama Prosecutor Found Guilty of Abusing Position for Sex."[29]

"China hands down terms of life to 8 years for sports officials convicted of taking bribes."[30]

I could list hundreds of recent headlines related to corruption. Even worse, the lack of integrity isn't just limited to business, government, and sports—it's pervasive everywhere. The subjects in the above headlines wanted to achieve something (*what*), but the way (*how*) they achieved the intended results lacked honesty and betrayed trust.

Integrity is often discussed, but here's the rub: it's rarely practiced. The daily headlines reveal that integrity isn't just a leadership checkbox; it's the difference between lasting impact and fleeting success. Integrity matters. It's imperative to your leadership. It will help you stand out in a world that too often celebrates cutting corners.

What's integrity? It's showing up the same way in every setting, without putting on a different mask for different rooms. It's about staying true to your word and following through, time after time.

Integrity means making the tough, right choices, even if nobody would notice if you took a shortcut. But you will.

Are you willing to do the right thing even when no one is watching? What about when they are?

Take the story of Andy Roddick during the 2005 Rome Masters tennis match. Roddick was just a point away from winning the match when his opponent hit a serve that was called out. Everyone was watching. How would Roddick react? Rather than take the victory, Roddick pointed out that the ball had actually clipped the line. He sacrificed an almost certain win to do what was right, and it ultimately cost him the match. But what Roddick gained was far more valuable—he became a symbol of old-fashioned sportsmanship, someone whose integrity transcended the game itself.[31] Something to be celebrated.

When you make a commitment, large or small, people are watching to see if your actions match your words. That's the essence of integrity: following through, even when it's inconvenient, even when it costs you. Because leadership without integrity is a house of cards, one gust away from collapsing.

But that's not all. Integrity is the cornerstone of leadership. With it, people will gladly follow and offer their best ideas. Without it, well, you know how that turns out.

As the authors of *The Leadership Challenge* observed, "It's clear that if people anywhere are willing to follow someone—whether it's into battle or the boardroom, in the front office or on the production floor—they first want to be sure that the individual is worthy of their trust... No matter what the setting, people want to be fully confident in their leaders, and to be fully confident, they have to believe that their leaders are individuals of authentic character and solid *integrity*."[32] (emphasis added)

You can't be just about what you accomplish – your ends – without being about how you achieve them – your how. For it is how you achieve results that mark you as having integrity. In this day and age, when so many achieve results by taking shortcuts and making moral compromises, integrity separates those who build to last from those who build only for the moment.

Integrity means being consistent, honest, and courageous enough to stick by your principles, even if it means losing your job, a friend, or a tennis match. It's how you will be remembered as a leader, and integrity is the essential starting point for being a good one.

NO TRUST, NO TEAM: BUILDING BRIDGES WITH INTEGRITY

Trust follows integrity. It's simple: keep your promises, stand up for others, and share the credit, and you'll earn trust. But betray people, take shortcuts, or grab someone else's spotlight, and you lose that trust just as quickly.

Trust is at the core of all personal and professional relationships. With it, you can accomplish great things in collaboration with others. Without it, you'll go nowhere.

Do you remember a time when trust was absent or broken? I do. Early in my Coke career, I worked with a group of people (not a real team), and we were going nowhere fast. Our manager (not a leader) was a self-serving individual, more worried about making a great impression with upper management. Unsurprisingly, our group was filled with dissension and gossip. We lacked priorities and direction. Our roles weren't clear. Our business partner didn't understand or value our contribution. We were distracted by an underperforming co-worker who created a drag on the group's overall effectiveness. There was no recognition of our hard work, let alone a pat on the back for a job well done. Trust was nowhere to be found.

After several co-workers left or were let go, I found myself being the only one that our manager could rely on to get things done. The burden became very heavy. Combined with a suffocating environment, overwork, and a lack of appreciation, I started to burn out.

I was doing everything I could to be a positive influence, but I was met with resistance around every corner. I began to lose hope that things would get better. I remember feeling broken and desperate. I was ready to leave the Company.

Then, I recall praying and sharing my circumstances with God. Novel idea, I know. I got the sense that I should *hold on*. I wasn't sure what *hold on* meant or why. However, at that moment, I resolved to take things one day at a time and not give up.

The next day was my birthday. When I arrived at work, my manager called me into her office and delivered the news. She was relocating to another city, and I'd soon have a new manager.

I can still recall the rush of relief that washed over me. *What a great birthday present!* I thought. A new hope. There was light at the end of the tunnel—and it wasn't an oncoming train. I was instantly optimistic about the future.

A few weeks later, I was appointed to a new team and assigned a new leader.

Yes, a *team* and a *leader* – a huge difference.

Immediately, my new manager, Mike, came to visit me and conduct my annual review. He was known throughout the company as a man of integrity and a great leader, someone whose word was as solid as his actions. His reputation preceded him, and it was this very quality that made me both hopeful and cautious as I joined his team. But in that moment, I was more than cautious; I was scared. My former manager completed the review document before she transferred, but it was Mike's responsibility to facilitate the discussion. I imagined the document contained more than enough reasons to run me off. I kept hearing in my mind, *You're fired. You're fired. Prepare yourself. You're fired!*

Mike held the review in his hand as we began our interaction. He told me that he disagreed with my former manager's assessment, and he acknowledged the hostile work environment in which I'd suffered. *Ah, what a relief!* Despite the circumstances, he said I was still recognized as a top performer, he believed in me, and he wanted me to be part of his new team. Mike set down the review document, looked me in the eye, and told me that what my former manager wrote didn't matter now. Then, he asked me if I wanted a fresh start and invited me to his new team kickoff in Atlanta. I eagerly nodded yes and thanked him for inviting me.

Upon my arrival at the kickoff, I recall having mixed feelings as I sat around a conference table with the new team. My past experience led me to doubt that strong leadership and teamwork were possible. I needed to see the proof in the pudding.

And the proof began...

Mike went first by sharing about his family, values, experiences, and his passion for the University of Tennessee. He asked for volunteers—pun intended (that's a college football reference for the unfamiliar)—to share something about themselves with the team. As folks opened up, I was amazed at everyone's vulnerability and the sense of personal connection. We laughed a bunch.

Then, Mike transitioned to discuss his team vision. He handed out a piece of paper that outlined the team's values, direction, destination, and expectations. As a team, we discussed and aligned with the proposed vision. Then, he encouraged us to focus on others, not ourselves, to serve rather than to be served. He emphasized teamwork, prioritization, fun—and, most of all, trust.

Yes, trust.

I hadn't been in a trusting environment for a while. It'd been dog-eat-dog for so long. But Mike's approach inspired me to follow him and become a team player.

During the next two years, the words on that vision page came to life. The time was some of the most enjoyable and memorable of my career. Our team collaborated, built strong partnerships, had a lot of fun, achieved great business results, and I grew by leaps and bounds.

For example, we hosted the NCAA Final Four, where I personally chauffeured Derek Whittenburg (member of the 1983 North Carolina State Men's Basketball national championship team) to events, hung out with American Idol's Ryan Seacrest, and attended a Maroon 5 concert with the team. To top it off, our business performance results were so strong that we won a Disney World incentive for all of our families. Because of trust, we achieved more together than we could have apart.

At the end of my time on Mike's team, I sent him a note that said, "I didn't think it was possible to work for an inspiring leader and trust others like I do now. You did what you said you'd do. You've restored my ability to trust. Thank you for believing in me and giving me a fresh start." Mike's been a friend and mentor ever since.

I asked Mike the other day about his memory of the circumstances and his role. He told me, "My view of the situation was that it was the team and each person who did the heavy lifting and hard work to make things happen. I only helped facilitate and enable great people to do great work together." Again, this exemplifies his humility and leadership.

If you're ever faced with an opportunity to build or restore trust, I recommend these approaches.

Be Real. Let others know who you are, your values, and what you stand for. Share your dreams, passions, desires, goals, experiences, successes, and failures. Go first and let go. Risk vulnerability with others, and they will reciprocate.

Establish Credibility. Be who you say you are. Do what you say you will do.

Embody integrity. Ensure that the audio matches the video – that your actions match your words. Follow through. Earn respect by helping others solve problems. Put people first.

Enable Collaboration. Create an environment where people feel safe, where failure and learning are valued, where opinions and ideas are openly shared, and where team members must rely on one another to achieve success.

Employ patience. Does your team seem reluctant? I've felt that way many times in my career. Before you expect your team to trust, you must trust the process. You must believe that integrity, transparency, and honesty are essential for building trust. There are no shortcuts. Put more bluntly, you are directly responsible for the level of trust in your organization because you are responsible for personal integrity.

Trust is the bridge between leadership and those who choose to follow. It's not built through grand speeches or lofty promises but through consistent, everyday actions rooted in integrity. Instead of focusing on building trust, Mike concentrated on living with integrity-doing what he said he would do. He didn't just claim to be a leader of integrity—he demonstrated it, turning words into actions that aligned with his values. His unwavering commitment to honesty and consistency transformed a broken team into one united by trust.

Don't worry about building trust; build integrity, and trust will follow.

Frankly, I don't recall many of the details of what we accomplished as a team. But *how* we did it is as clear as if it happened yesterday.

PRINCIPLE
Be integrous, and trust will follow

QUESTIONS

How do you respond when your integrity is tested in the workplace?

Reflect on a time when you faced an ethical dilemma. Did you uphold your values, or did you compromise? What did you learn from that experience, and how can you apply those lessons to future challenges?

_____

_____

_____

In what ways does your daily behavior build or erode trust with your team and colleagues?

Consider your actions, words, and decisions. Are they consistent with the principles of integrity? How might small changes in your approach enhance the trust others place in you?

_____

_____

_____

What steps can you take to reinforce your commitment to integrity, even in the face of adversity? (Or, as Mark Twain rightly encouraged us, to "astonish" those around you.)

We often speak negatively about someone needing a "crutch." Unless, of course, we're talking about someone with a weak, injured, or missing leg. Think about growing in integrity this way. In what areas is your past practice of integrity weak? To grow stronger in integrity, what "crutches" would help you grow, heal, and walk straight?

CHAPTER 6

Titles Don't Matter

"It's not the will to win that matters—everybody has that.
It's the will to prepare to win that matters."

—COACH BEAR BRYANT

Did you know that you'll influence at least 10,000 people during your lifetime,[33] Even the most introverted person, like me, can impact up to 10,000 people—for good or bad. If you're an extrovert or have more engagement with people, this number only grows. The more you grow as a leader, the more you realize that your ability to influence others for good will become perhaps the greatest satisfaction of your career or life. Sounds like significance to me.

But here's the challenge. How do you lead when you don't have formal authority? How do you inspire someone to act because they *want* to, not because they have to? That's where influence comes in.

Influence is defined as "the power to have an important effect on someone or something. If someone influences someone else, they are changing a person or thing in an indirect but important way."[34] The Latin root of influence means "to flow in." So, when you influence, you're flowing into somebody or something. I've always used the definition that influence is *leadership without the crutch of authority*. When you don't have the authority to make things happen directly (what) and must work with and through other people to deliver results (how), you want influence.

Influence isn't a luxury; it's a necessity. In fact, influencing others is considered one of the top five skills needed in the future workplace.[35] In today's complex business landscape, the ability to influence others is the difference between leaders who merely manage and those who inspire change.

A recent study found that 61% of executives surveyed considered influencing a critical skill to develop, yet only 28% had received formal training in this area.[36] This disconnect highlights a significant opportunity—and responsibility—for leaders to cultivate these skills, ensuring they can lead effectively, even without formal authority.

Often, I tell people the best way to develop their influencing skills, if they're not in a leadership or management capacity, is to take a leadership position at a nonprofit or volunteer organization. People there typically won't report directly to you, and money is often not a motivating factor, so you have to collaborate and influence them on a human level. *What a concept, right?*

It's a myth that leadership is all about having authority and a title. Real leadership is about making an impact, exerting influence, and inspiring others.

TURNING ADVERSITY INTO ADVANTAGE

After completing my short-term developmental stint with Hershey's Sales Development department, I was anxiously awaiting my next assignment. I'd invested two years learning everything about the confection business and knew that my new role could be anywhere in the United States.

The phone rang. "Hi, Preston. This is Dave. We'd like you to become the Giant-Carlisle key account manager and stay in the Hershey area."

My heart sank, and my forehead began dripping with beads of sweat because I'd heard how difficult it was to call on Giant. *Do I have what it takes?* I asked myself.

Dave continued, "Your role won't be easy at first. As you know, Giant is in our backyard. A majority of our employees shop in Giant's stores. You'll be under a microscope."

Microscope? I imagined thousands of Hershey employees lined up outside my new office, complaining about something. *There's no product on the shelf. Pricing is wrong. Why don't you move the display closer to the front of the store? Wah wah wah!*.

Add to this the fact that our company had a lot of baggage with Giant. "Things haven't gone well with them over the past few years. We'll want you to 'bend the trend,' restore relationships, turn the business around, and deliver results. Are you up to the challenge?"

With a lump in my throat, I vacillated over the opportunity. *Is this really what I want? Why me? What did I do to deserve this? Talk about career-limiting moves.* Pushing my doubts and fears aside, I blurted, "Yes."

"Great and welcome aboard. I've already set up a meeting with Giant's confectionary buyer… tomorrow! I'll brief you on the way to the meeting."

Boy, this will be a quick transition. It'll be sink or swim. Bend the trend or be bent.

On the car ride to our appointment, Dave briefed me on Giant and Sam, the candy category buyer. He told me that Sam was one of the most stringent buyers in the Northeast. In his opinion, Sam was egotistical, demanding, and hard to get along with. He was ambitious and only approved innovation or promotions that made him look good. No one at Hershey had been able to make a significant breakthrough with him.

The two companies' relationship was purely transactional, with little hope of developing a strategic one. To complicate matters, our key competitor took advantage of Hershey's challenges with Sam. It didn't look good having them beat us in our home market. No pressure.

As we sat down with Sam for lunch, you could cut the tension with a knife. Right off, Sam was defensive and began telling us about the issues with Hershey's customer service. I gripped my chair and clenched my teeth. *Don't respond, be cool.* He said we had great brands, but we didn't deliver on promises.

The conversation then turned to the "baggage" Dave mentioned. Giant made big plans to promote Hershey's brands during last year's Halloween season. However, Hershey couldn't deliver the product due to an untimely SAP data platform conversion; multiple candy truckloads were "lost" in the system and never made it to Giant's warehouses. Giant lost millions of dollars in sales. Sam felt burned—personally. As a result, he didn't receive an incentive, and he'd lost favor in management's eyes. Things weren't so sweet.

After lunch, Sam looked me in the eye and said, "I'm not sure you want this role. I'm not going to be of any help to you or Hershey."

I smiled, trying to hide my nerves, and said, "Well, Sam, you're probably right. I'm not sure I want it either! But here we are, and I don't back down from a challenge. So how about we give this a shot and see what we can do together?" I figured a little humor and humility might break the ice. Sam just shrugged. On top of all that, he left me with the check without saying thank you.

As Dave and I drove back to the office, something unexpected happened. Instead of being fearful, I embraced the challenge. I figured that if I could somehow break through with Sam, we could turn everything around.

I began with a series of short sales calls to connect with Sam. I asked him questions about Giant's strategy, operating model, and what mattered to him. I listened to him with an open mind and curiosity for solutions.

After learning what was important to Giant and Sam, I began proposing promotions or new item opportunities that aligned with Giant's strategy. Over the next few weeks, he said "no" to me so many times I lost count. I felt frustrated but determined. Sam continued to keep me on the sidelines because of the previous year's Halloween delivery debacle. To prove his point, Sam ordered only 10% of his regular Halloween candy. The small order put our business in a huge hole, and I needed to figure out a way out of it.

The promotional ideas didn't seem to be working, so I decided to take a different approach. I invited Sam and his girlfriend to a Washington Redskins football game. Why? Sam told me that he was a huge Redskins fan, but he had never been to a football game in DC.

I secured four company tickets in the second row. My wife and I rented a chauffeured limousine, picked up Sam and his girlfriend, and made our way to the stadium. Sam wore his Redskins jersey and was like a kid in a candy store (pun intended). I was very intentional about not bringing up business during our conversations, as I genuinely wanted to connect with him on a personal level.

Shortly after we arrived at our seats, Sam brought up business. He told me that I'd been on the bench too long. "Nothing personal," he said. He'd seen how hard I'd tried and really appreciated some of the business opportunities I'd shared. I asked him what it would take to turn our business around and restore the relationship between Giant and Hershey. His answer was striking in its clarity.

"Do what you say you'll do."

I responded, "Okay, I'll do everything in my power to deliver. With that in mind, what can I deliver?"

We began brainstorming ideas for a game-changing promotion that would benefit both companies. He shared best practices other manufacturers used to help grow Giant's business. I listened to all of his ideas, and we aligned on a plan. I asked him if Hershey delivered on our collaborative concept, would Giant be aligned? Sam answered, "Yes."

I collaborated with my cross-functional team to develop a "How the Grinch Stole Christmas" movie tie-in and partnership with Coca-Cola. We created a shopper marketing program before shopper marketing was cool. The program included joint point of sale (POS), in-store merchandising, an exclusive movie premiere, and supporting radio promotions. The plan's execution would grow his business and align with Giant's strategies. The proposal met all of the promotion elements we discussed. There was only one item that remained.

I threw a Hail Mary and asked for an unprecedented order that would quadruple his Holiday candy order compared to last year. If agreed, the order would overcome the Halloween deficit and put Hershey over our annual goal. Sam didn't hesitate. "Okay. Write a suggested store-level order and have it to me by next week." Touchdown.

"One other thing," he glared. "You'd better deliver!"

I confidently replied, "We'll do what we said we'll do."

And we did. The promotion was a smashing success. Giant and Hershey both exceeded their annual business plan. It was gratifying to play a role in bending the performance trend and restoring relationships. Additionally, my team won Hershey's prestigious "President's Cup" for achieving the highest sales performance in the company compared to the prior year. Best of all, Sam got promoted.

You might be thinking, *Really, Preston? Buy your clients and team members football tickets and a Limo ride, and that will create influence?*

Nope. It wasn't the football game that created influence; it was my consistency in keeping my promise. The game only allowed a conversation; the influence started building the day Sam and I met. Even though my repeated attempts to bring win-win ideas to the table seemed to fumble, he was keeping score. (That's all the football puns… for now.) Through it all, I learned that the how—understanding what truly mattered to Sam—was the key to building lasting influence.

How did that promotion turn out for me? Well, that's a story for later on. Let's just say that bending the trend sometimes comes with a price.

IF YOU CAN'T BEAT 'EM, HARNESS 'EM

Influence reaches its full potential when it brings people together, turning individual efforts into a unified force.

The anticipated announcement was made: The Coca-Cola Company agreed to purchase two competitive companies, Glaceau (which includes Vitaminwater and Smartwater) and Fuze Beverages. The incoming water and juice brands were fantastic and complementary acquisitions to our existing hydration beverage portfolio. However, the acquisitions came with complications and created internal competition. Each acquired company had its own sales team and its own plans. My role was similar, with a focus on my company's legacy brands.

During my tenure, I'd established strong relationships with the bottler. However, my influence slowly eroded as the new sales teams began integrating. The new team members leveraged exciting incentives, expensive dinners, and premiums to woo the bottler. Excluding me, they tied up meeting times and market visits. Our mutual bottling partner became enamored with the shiny new penny and lost sight of the ball.

Execution of all the legacy brands began to slip, and total sales stagnated. I discovered that the newly acquired business contributed only 10% of the total bottler's revenue, while all the legacy brands I represented accounted for 90%. I determined that our problem boiled down to focus; if we didn't recalibrate our focus on the 90%, we wouldn't make the plan. At the same time, we needed the newly acquired brands to flourish.

The only solution I could think of was to fight fire with fire. I'd need to double my efforts. Get back in the game with more attractive incentives, fancy dinners, and premiums to woo the bottler's attention back. I wasn't entirely comfortable with this approach, but I believed there had to be a solution somewhere. I just didn't know where.

I was stuck.

I prayed to God and asked for wisdom to meet the challenge and identify a game-changing solution.

Then it happened. Inspiration struck like a bolt of lightning while watching my all-time favorite movie, the 1959 Academy Award-winning *Ben-Hur*. There's a scene where the movie's main character, Judah Ben-Hur, is observing a chariot race practice. The chariot was pulled by a team of four strong and fast horses. Just before the chariot approached a curve, Ben-Hur commented that the chariot would never make the turn. And he was right.

The horses ran straight through the turn and off the track. When asked how he knew that the chariot would run off course, Ben-Hur told the owner that he raced in the Roman circus. Based on his experience, he observed that the horses were strong and fast, but they weren't positioned to leverage their individual strengths. They were running as individuals, not as a single unit. Ben-Hur rearranged the horses, placing the slower, steadier horse on the inside to anchor the team during turns and the faster horse on the outside. The owner said, "Show me."

To the owner's amazement, Ben-Hur raced the chariot around the track in record time without incident. The parallel was striking. We have a strong team of people representing our brands to the bottler. I wondered, "What if we worked together and everyone achieved their goals? What if I harnessed the team, positioned them by strength and we ran as one?"

Said another way, if you can't beat them, join them.

None of the new team members reported to me, so I had to rely entirely on influence to align everyone's efforts. I invited fifteen new brand and bottler representatives to a groundbreaking "Brand Partner Summit." Our objective was to build trust, establish open lines of communication, initiate collaborative planning, facilitate execution, and, above all, eliminate internal competition. After all, we were now one company and should be focused on a unified race against our true competitors.

The meeting's theme was "Running as One." We began our time together horseback riding in the Smoky Mountains—a chance for everyone to connect outside the office and get acquainted. After the team-building exercise, we gathered for a dinner on roles and responsibilities. All of the individuals shared how they added value to the company. The next day, I opened the Summit with the Ben-Hur chariot practice movie clip and asked the team to consider how we begin to run as one. Participants started making connections and collaboration recommendations as we reviewed each other's business updates, priorities, and plans.

Ultimately, the Brand Partners concluded that our initiatives needed to be integrated into a comprehensive monthly Sales Plan. The Sales Plan captured and communicated all execution priorities, allowing Brand Partners and our bottling partner to be on the same page.

The Sales Plan solution mitigated internal competition, improved collaboration, and ensured that everyone met their business plan. We ran as one. It wasn't just the what—the plan itself—that made the difference, but how we worked together to develop and execute it to such an extent that our Brand Partner Summit and Sales Plan were deemed best practices and adopted by other parts of the company.

STRATEGIC INFLUENCE: EARNING YOUR SEAT AT THE TABLE

A few years ago, I attended a team reunion in San Destin, Florida. It was an excellent time to reflect on one of my favorite periods in my career. Why? As a team, we accomplished great things. Personally, I was considered a strategic business partner and was given the authority to make a difference. Before I tell you about the reunion, let me provide some context.

In 2001, I served as my company's representative in Montgomery, Alabama, where I was responsible for delivering positive business results with the local bottler. The family-owned operation was recently acquired by a more massive bottler. When the new bottler took over operations, the transition didn't go smoothly. Based on missed deliveries, inferior execution, high turnover, and many broken promises, the new operators lost credibility with the customers and the community. Most of the original leadership team was released, and new leaders were assigned to clean up the mess.

I was part of the new leadership team assigned to turn things around and knew I was stepping into a challenging situation. The relationship between the company and its bottlers was tenuous. I knew that to become a trusted member of the team, I'd need to win their hearts by investing time with the bottler's leaders and connecting with them personally. I started by learning about the local market, taking trade rides to gain a sense of what the frontline associates needed, asking numerous questions, listening, and sharing a meal together. Chewing loosens up those jaws and opens conversations, right?

I quickly realized that the new Montgomery market leaders were the real deal. To gain a seat at the table and align with them, I provided insights and value-creating solutions to help the business grow. I built credibility with the team leader, and over time, I was entrusted to develop and drive the local market strategy, as well as steward key marketing asset relationships (e.g., the University of Alabama and Auburn University). I'd moved from just aligning with the bottler's leadership team to becoming their strategic business partner.

How? Through being trustworthy, sharing a common purpose, promoting transparency, being humble, and always maintaining a sense of humor when things get tough. After considerable effort, our team's execution improved significantly, and our business results exceeded expectations. The team was nationally recognized for its efforts, and a number of us were promoted due to the successful market turnaround. Back to the reunion.

I was honored to be part of the San Destin festivities. There was only a handful of company representatives invited to the reunion, but I was the only one to attend. It was great to see all of the people. We hugged and shared fond memories. During dinner, about a dozen people stood up and shared funny stories about our time together. As we were going around the table, I realized that I'd be the last person to speak that evening. *What am I going to say that hasn't already been said?*

Then it hit me. Talk about *partnership*.

My current role had me in a position to influence strategic partnerships worldwide. In large part, being a strategic partner with my former teammates in the room equipped me for the work.

After a few opening comments, I expressed my gratitude. "Thank you for modeling what a successful partnership looks like. You embraced me and gave me a seat at your table. I can't tell you how much I appreciated it then, and I still do today."

"Why?" I continued, "I remember unifying phrases like, 'One team, one goal' or the many days traveling together to different sales centers where we got to know each other. We created shared values and a shared vision. Despite all the obstacles we encountered, we accomplished a great deal. The way you treated me and the partnership we developed modeled what success looks like. I'm leading a project that helps others in North America and around the globe build strategic partnerships—across Peru, Russia, the Philippines, and beyond. Who would have thought a rookie like me in a small market like Alabama would have an opportunity to make a worldwide impact?

Investing in the development of influence is not optional; it's essential. How do you become a strategic partner and an influential figure?

1. *Become Trustworthy*: Build credibility through doing what you say you'll do and adding value. Earn your seat at the table by providing thought leadership, developing solutions, and delivering results.
2. *Unify through a Common Purpose*: Clearly define where you're headed, the collective ways of working together, and what the partnership wants to achieve. Ultimately, partners want to improve their own business results.
3. *Promote Transparency:* Drive open and honest, two-way communication. Accept all feedback as a gift. When faced with problems or conflict, talk things out, remembering to always focus on the issue at hand, not the person.
4. *Be Humble:* Take the position of a servant. Think less about yourself and your goals and think more about how to help others.
5. *Keep a Sense of Humor:* Remember, laughter is the shortest distance between two people. Know when to interject humor into situations and put others at ease. (And don't drop the ball when it comes to football jokes.)

This reunion reminded me that the real success wasn't just what we achieved—it was how we did it. By fostering trust, transparency, and a shared purpose, we transformed a challenging situation into a lasting partnership. This approach not only delivered results but also created bonds that extended far beyond the workplace, proving that how we lead is what truly matters.

THE ONE ABOUT THE SQUEEZE

Sometimes in life, you make a move that is uncharacteristic but required.

I picked up the phone, dialed the number in trepidation, and asked for the president. The assistant on the other end said, "Please hold." Dramatic on-hold music played in the background. (Not really, but you get the idea.) "I'm connecting you now."

The conversation was one I'll never forget. But first, let me offer a brief backstory.

As I mentioned earlier, I started my career with The Coca-Cola Company (TCCC) in Montgomery, Alabama, in 2001. My mission was to collaboratively develop annual business plans with our bottling partners, align on direction, enable marketplace execution, and lead marketing asset relationships.

Marketing assets are a fantastic way to connect with consumers and serve as a source of pride for The Coca-Cola System (i.e., the Company and its bottling partners). The assets give Coca-Cola access to where consumers create memories and develop an emotional connection with the brand. What's an asset? In this context, examples are sporting events, concerts, or amusement parks. The goal is a positive association. Here are three things you should know about marketing assets.

Marketing assets are expensive. TCCC and its bottling partner typically split the investment. Hence, there was always a push to recoup the investment.

Marketing assets are hyper-competitive. Over time, we accumulated many strategic marketing assets. I always heard that we had an *embarrassment of riches*. But that meant our primary competitor was forever eager to convert an asset from red (i.e., Coke-owned) to blue (i.e., Pepsi-owned) when partnership agreements expired.

Marketing assets are exigent. Big word, I know. It means that business relationships *require attention.* Effective partnerships stem from being connected and creating mutually beneficial value. If the parties disconnect, one may take the other for granted, and engagements become transactional; the relationship will eventually erode.

Enter the #1 Marketing Asset

The University of Alabama was the number one marketing asset in the state of Alabama, and the Crimson Tide had a legendary partnership with Coca-Cola.

For example, Head Football Coach Bear Bryant used to drink Coca-Cola and eat Golden Flake potato chips during his weekly TV show. The ultimate product placement. And "Great Pair Says the Bear" was the ultimate product endorsement.

But after Coach Bryant retired and the University of Alabama Football program's success moderated, so did the relationship between Coca-Cola and the UA Athletic Department.

A head coach carousel ensued with names like Perkins, Curry, Dubose, Franchione, Price, and Shula.[37] But no one could restore Alabama Football glory. The only exception was Gene Stallings, who rebuilt the program, regained national prominence, and won the 1992 National Football Championship.

Simultaneously, Pepsi slowly and quietly built relationships behind the scenes with the University of Alabama's key stakeholders. And Pepsi improved its market share across the State of Alabama, making inroads with customers and consumers. Everything changed slowly—and then all at once. The tipping point came in 1998.

The Coca-Cola and UA pouring rights contract expired and went out to bid. Quite possibly the worst thing to happen to the current contract holder. It typically means that costs will rise, and it serves as a signal that relationships are strained. Pouring rights - they grant a supplier the right to provide beverages (fountain and bottled drinks) and marketing exclusivity in the sports venues.

Astonishingly, Pepsi secured the ten-year pouring rights contract despite its history with Coke. Then, Pepsi was shocked.

When they signed the pouring rights agreement, they assumed that the University would also award them the out-of-venue media (e.g., billboards, TV/radio commercials) and marketing rights (e.g., on-pack logo usage, imagine the UA logo on a 20 oz Coke bottle, and in-store promotions). Not so fast.

Fortunately, Coca-Cola had a separate contract with Crimson Tide Sports Marketing (CTSM) for marketing rights outside the stadium. CTSM managed things like game radio broadcasts and the weekly coaches' TV shows. They bought the rights to advertise outside the stadium from the University of Alabama and then sold those advertising opportunities to sponsors, including Coca-Cola.

The CTSM contract enabled Coke to maintain a relationship with UA and allowed our team to market the Coca-Cola and University of Alabama association. We were still in the game, but the marketing and media rights contract was about to expire soon. We needed to think and act fast because Pepsi would pay anything to secure the contract.

Our job was to show UA how Coca-Cola created value beyond just a big payment. We needed to flex our marketing muscle, which was our competitor's weakness.

A Bridge to the Future

In pre-strategy development meetings with UA, we discovered they were concerned about the next-generation Alabama fans. The football team's legacy was fading, and a nationwide survey found that Bear Bryant would all but be forgotten by the class of 2007. UA needed to establish relevance with younger consumers. We could help them do that and build a bridge to the future.

Our team developed a comprehensive, four-pronged marketing approach to connect with and recruit the next generation, focusing on four key levels: statewide, the City of Tuscaloosa, the University of Alabama campus, and game day. Our campaign slogan was "Tide Tradition." We presented the strategy and campaign to the UA Athletic Director, Assistant AD, and Head Football Coach. They loved it. They also wanted to see if we would execute it. That's when the fun began.

We launched a statewide Fall Football promotion with University of Alabama logos on Coca-Cola products and in-store displays. We also built partnerships with local businesses in Tuscaloosa, supported community events, established Coke vending and dining programs on campus, hired a student ambassador, and organized the "Coca-Cola Kickoff on the Quad," a fun game day event featuring activities such as inflatables, games, and free product samples.

The marketing strategy was successful. We literally changed the landscape. In fact, the plan was the first of its kind. It became the model for other College and University marketing activation nationwide. But one crucial element remained. The CTSM contract. Although the renewal was verbally awarded to us, it was never signed by the University. At any time, UA could have pulled the plug and awarded the media and marketing rights to Pepsi.

The Game-changer

A group of Coca-Cola executives, including myself, met with Dr. Robert Witt, the President of the University of Alabama. Our meeting agenda included sharing Coke's successful marketing strategy and how our partnership benefited the University. We also wanted to explore Dr. Witt's thoughts about the future and how we could help.

After an enthusiastic and productive conversation, Dr. Witt produced a 6-pack of Louisiana State University (LSU) Football

National Championship 8-oz glass bottles. He said the 6-pack was sent by LSU's president, reminding Dr. Witt of LSU's recent accomplishment. Dr. Witt paused and said, "I want to bring both of these back to the University of Alabama, a national football championship and Coca-Cola into Bryant-Denny stadium where it belongs."

Then, Dr. Witt revealed a surprise. His nephew was employed at Coca-Cola. "He's your campus ambassador and is having a wonderful experience. Thank you for all that you're teaching him."

Wow. I had no idea we'd hired Dr. Witt's nephew. Another moment of serendipity.

Dr. Witt concluded our conversation with an appreciation for the historic partnership between UA and Coca-Cola, as well as what we were doing to build a bridge to the future. "If you ever need anything, just call."

Six months went by. I continued to press CTSM, the UA Assistant Athletic Director, and the University General Counsel to sign the agreement. Continual barriers and delays. It seemed as if some backroom deal with Pepsi was in the works. I felt responsible for securing the contract so we could all move on.[38]

Then it hit me. Why not call Dr. Witt and take him up on his offer to help? I was aware of the political damage that going over the heads of key stakeholders might cause. Time to take a risk.

"Hello, this is Bob Witt. How can I help you?"

I re-introduced myself and told Dr. Witt about our challenge with the contract signature delay. He said he understood and would call me back in ten minutes.

More imaginary dramatic music. I was sure I'd overstepped my boundaries and would aggravate my constituents. Bottling Partner leadership won't look kindly on my approach. University personnel will call for my replacement. I may be demoted or even fired.

Nine minutes later, the phone rang. With a frog in my throat, I answered, "Hello."

"Preston, Bob Witt again. I talked to the University General Counsel, the contract will be signed today, and final copies will be sent to you immediately."

I replied, "Terrific, and thanks for your help. I spent almost two years working to have the contract signed. It only took you ten minutes."

What Dr. Witt said next always stuck with me.

"Sometimes you just gotta squeeze 'em by the balls."

Influence comes in many forms, I suppose.

The signed contract arrived the next day. And I never faced any repercussions for going around the key stakeholders of the UA.

That was the last time I talked to Dr. Witt before moving to my next role. I'll always look back fondly on those times. Not only did the Coke team outmaneuver our competition and secure the media and marketing rights, but we also created a beachhead for a future team to eventually regain exclusive athletic venue pouring, campus dining, and vending, and marketing rights in 2018.

THE LONG GAME: INFLUENCE TAKES TIME TO GROW

Position sometimes matters. Influence is leadership without the crutch of authority. But influence has its limitations. While I'd established credibility and grown my influence with UA's key stakeholders, no amount of influence seemed to matter. Dr. Witt had the authority to make things happen with just one short phone call.

Persistence pays off. It took two years from the day the verbal agreement was received to the day the contract was consummated. And it took another fifteen years for Coke to restore its storied relationship with UA. The team's persistence paid off. If we didn't fight hard to create the beachhead for the next group to advance the relationship, the campus and city would have indeed turned blue. And Coke would have missed what the future held: Nick Saban and six National Football Championships.

Providence plays out. I referred to providence as serendipity. But events like Coke retaining the marketing rights, even though Pepsi thought they secured them, or unknowingly hiring Dr. Witt's relative as our campus ambassador, went beyond mere chance. The hand of providence played out.

Like winning, influence isn't about the desire to lead or control but about the groundwork you lay beforehand. Just as Coach Bryant said, "It's the will to *prepare* to win that matters." My influence with Dr. Witt didn't stem from a single phone call; it developed over years of building credibility, trust, and strong relationships. When the moment came to make that game-changing call, it was the preparation—*how* I had conducted myself over time—that made all the difference. Influence, like winning, is earned through consistent effort.

Think of influence like a tree. Which has more impact, a pine sapling or a giant sequoia? And like trees, it takes time, experience, and steadfastness to grow. But eventually, people take note, and the influence is undeniable. Take another look at the diagram below. Like the rings of a tree, influential leadership is built layer by layer, and that's why the progression is so crucial for our growth.

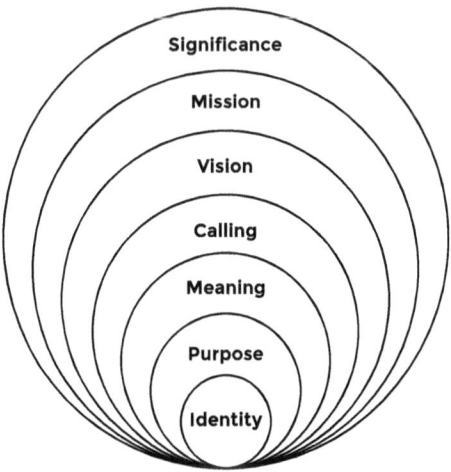

There are no shortcuts to creating influence. Start today by doing what you say you'll do and communicating along the way. Lay the groundwork for the game-changing phone call you'll need to make five years from now.

PRINCIPLE

Build influence brick by brick

QUESTIONS

How can you use your influence to inspire action in your current role, even when you don't have formal authority?

_____
_____
_____

In what ways can you strengthen your influence with your current team or colleagues? Are there specific relationships you need to nurture or strategies you need to adjust?

_____
_____
_____

Are you doing what you've said you'll do with those around you? Where can you course-correct? Who do you need to talk to and admit where you've dropped the ball?

_____
_____
_____

CHAPTER 7

Dancing with Wolves

> "Courage is being scared to death but saddling up anyway. "
>
> – JOHN WAYNE

Panicked by the rapid footsteps closing in behind me, I began sprinting as fast as I could. My heart was racing, my chest tightened, and I struggled to breathe. A pack of wolves was chasing me. The alpha male had targeted me for some reason, and I was the pack's prey. Maybe they sensed weakness or vulnerability. The pack chased me for what felt like an eternity, and I could feel they were about to catch me.

I dripped with sweat, fearful of what was about to happen but too exhausted to continue. In an instant, the lead wolf had me. Amazingly, I found the strength to fight back and somehow escape. My injuries took a long time to heal, and so did my fears. I couldn't shake my experience with the alpha male and his pack. Wherever I went, I was always fearful that another pack of wolves was waiting to ambush me. So, I made the decision to never reveal my weaknesses or vulnerabilities. I didn't want to become a target again.

OKAY, IT'S METAPHORICAL

During my last year at Hershey Chocolate, I was targeted by Mal Boss and his pack of wolves. Mal was the Sales VP and was an intimidating figure. He had wolf-like features: one blue eye and another green, gray hair, and a skin color to match. His ears were always on alert, sensing opportunities to pounce on someone. Call him "The Wolf of Chocolate Street." It was his way or the highway. If you didn't conform to his methods, your career at Hershey would be over.

At first, Mal liked me. I graduated from the Sales Development program, a two-year Hershey boot camp for high-potential individuals, and was assigned as the Hershey market key account manager. I excelled in the Sales Development role, and Mal appreciated my aggressive and results-driven nature.

But I was overconfident and made some political mistakes early on. For example, I was assigned to call on Giant Foods Headquarters in Carlisle, PA, just outside Hershey. Because of the headquarters' proximity to the town of Hershey, several Hershey Chocolate executives, including Mal Boss, were involved in the account. Giant Foods management told me they wanted me to be the sole point of contact; "too many cooks in the chocolate factory," they said. Mal didn't like the idea, but he agreed to withdraw from the account and see what would happen.

I was authorized to make decisions with Giant Foods management. We implemented vital product selection and promotion changes, but Mal disagreed with the decisions. And he held a grudge against me for withdrawing from the account. That's when the chase began.

During meetings, he'd publicly challenge and demean me in front of my peers. I stopped being invited to crucial Hershey meetings. He pulled all administrative support. Mal personally reviewed all of my expense reports, looking for any discrepancies. Then, his pack began to surround me.

Hershey, PA, is a small town. When my family lived there, the population was 12,000 people, and 5,000 of them worked for

Hershey. Every new product launch or promotion execution was there for everyone to see—the good and the bad. If something were wrong, I'd get the call to fix it. The scrutiny became more intense as Mal encouraged his pack to contact me if something was amiss. And they did.

I worked even harder, hoping that my performance and results would speak for themselves. However, it eventually reached the point where it seemed I couldn't do anything right. The pack was in my head at this point. My negative self-talk was deafening, and the stress was overwhelming. I remember getting a twitch in my right eye that wouldn't stop. I was scared of losing my job, frightened of failure, afraid of letting my young family down, and worried I'd be unemployable. I was in a doom loop and felt hopeless.

Fear is triggered when you anticipate physical harm or a perceived threat. Fear elicits physical responses, such as sweating, a rapid heartbeat, and feelings of weakness. Fright also evokes apathy, inaction, and ignorance. Chronic fear can impact your overall well-being. Studies show that top fears include failure, success (yes, really), dying, commitment, public speaking, rejection, making the wrong decision, criticism, taking responsibility, and the unknown. (Aside from dying, which of those don't leaders face daily?)

I learned a long time ago that fear stands for False Evidence Appearing Real, meaning that one's perceptions drive negative emotions and thinking. For example, everyone engages in a daily conversation with themselves. Studies show that we have "12,000 to 60,000 thoughts per day, and as many as 98 percent of them are exactly the same as we had the day before."[39] This self-talk is often damaging. As a matter of fact, eight out of ten thoughts we have each day are negative. Do the math. That's up to 48,000 negative thoughts daily.[40] Don't believe me? Think about the lies you tell yourself every day. Have you ever found yourself thinking:

I am unworthy.

I can't lead.
I am a failure.
I'm not good enough.
No one loves me or cares for me.
I don't belong anywhere.
I have no purpose.
I'm weak.
This will never work.
I must be perfect.
It's too late to pursue my dream.

With all the negative thoughts, where do you turn? How do you overcome fear? I took a moment to reflect and found an inner resolve. I began replacing negative self-talk with positive affirmations. I reminded myself of my strengths, my capabilities, and my past successes.

Gradually, I found the courage to pull things together and put an exit plan in place. I began working with an executive recruiter and eventually landed my dream job with The Coca-Cola Company. Our family moved back to the Southeast, and my salary increased by 30%! The experience taught me that overcoming fear is less about eliminating it and more about learning to manage it.

Through the interview process, I realized that my challenging experiences at Hershey had actually prepared me to secure my new role. But I was still recovering from Mal Boss and the wolf pack attacks. For years, I didn't trust upper management. Out of self-preservation, I wouldn't say much in front of them. And when I did, I'd stutter and stammer through my comments, just waiting to be challenged or embarrassed.

It took a long time to heal these wounds and overcome my fears. It wasn't easy. Over time, I began to see that not everyone was out to get me. In fact, most people were out to help me.

DEALING WITH FEAR

The answer is not in getting rid of fear but in how you handle it. Fear is an emotion, and as humans, we all fear something. Even leaders have fears. Where do you go when the negative thoughts come knocking at your door? How do you deal with fear?

- *Own Your Fear.* Yes, it is scary. So are thunderstorms, but you don't have to stand in the rain. You can own it without letting it own you.
- *Talk Positively to Yourself.* If you wouldn't let someone speak to you that way, why let your brain do it? Be your own hype person. Think of it as a pre-game pep talk and TED Talk.
- *Seek Support.* Even Batman had Alfred. Don't try to be a solo hero. Find your people and get the wisdom you need.
- *Develop a Plan.* Winging it works great for birds, but for the rest of us? Not so much. Write the plan, then work on the plan.
- *Act.* Fear doesn't take a day off, so you've got to clock in too. Start small. Rome wasn't built in a day, and neither is your confidence.

Here are some affirmations to replace your negative self-talk:
Because of my capabilities, I am worthy.
I can lead.
I am successful.
I'm good enough.
I'm loved and cared for.
I do belong.
I have a purpose.
I'm strong.
This will work.
I can make mistakes.
It's never too late to pursue my dream.

Fear is contagious; a follower will not support or commit to you if they sense fear in you. Courage is also contagious, and people will follow you if they feel that you possess courage.

Courage does not mean being fearless – it means moving forward despite fear. How you break through the fear is what defines the leader. That's the heart of the How>What philosophy. It's not about avoiding the storm but about how you navigate through it.

PUNCHLINES AND PANIC: LESSONS IN FACING FEAR

Speaking of comfort zones, it's one thing to step out of them; it's another to leap headfirst into what feels like a lion's den—or, in my case, a comedy club. If you want to test your ability to stay cool under pressure, try getting a crowd of 200 people, including friends and family, to laugh at your jokes. Spoiler alert: I took the leap, and let's just say it wasn't a soft landing.

The self-talk begins with "don't forget your lines," "don't trip," and "don't embarrass yourself." However, after thousands of presentations in my career, I've learned to adjust my self-talk to focus on positive thoughts, such as "you've practiced and earned the right to be here," "enjoy the moment," and "don't be hard on yourself when you mess up."

But this time was different. I'd never performed a stand-up comedy routine in front of a live audience—200 paying customers, including 20 family members and friends expecting to laugh.

I took three deep breaths. Then, I heard, "Let's give a round of applause for Preston Poh...Pohr...Preston Poore..."

Here goes nothing. I bounced on stage and delivered my opening line, "Hi, I'm Preston Poore, *poor* like no money with an 'E' on the end." My first joke. Who would have ever thought I'd perform a comedy routine at Atlanta's The Punchline?

I've long been interested in learning the ins and outs of writing and delivering humorous content. It all began when I saw an Atlanta

Journal-Constitution article on Jeff Justice's Comedy Workshoppe. He'd been teaching comedic skills for thirty years and had roughly 3,000 people graduate from his class. Over the years, I've developed the ability to tell stories that stir every human emotional reaction—except laughter. Let's say I'm better at drama than comedy; a little intense and less laid back. I wanted to improve my ability to relate and connect with others.

Laughter enables human connection and accelerates bonding. Impromptu jokes among friends and family come easily to me. But I lacked confidence in intentionally tickling someone's funny bone. During the Comedy Workshoppe, I discovered that comedy is serious business, both an art and a science. Over the course of six weeks, I discovered my sense of humor and learned how to convey it effectively.

Here's how the process worked. During each session, I was required to read a joke I'd written to Jeff and my twenty fellow participants. Jeff then provided feedback on how to improve the joke. I'd go home, integrate the input, rewrite the original joke, and create a new one. Then, the process began all over again.

For example, here's the first joke I wrote about tipping:

"I'm a little offended by the COVID-era touchscreen payment systems. You know, the ones where you can tip before your meal, 18%, 20%, 25%, and you're forced to choose. Ever notice there's rarely a 'no tip' option? It's like they're hustling me. How about adding a 'Isn't a tip premature right now?' option... or a 'How dare you!' option . . . or a 'Just give me my food and please don't spit in it' option?"

Here's the final joke after Jeff and his team's input:

"Tonight, I was placing my order at Chipotle, and the cashier twisted the screen around, expecting a tip. *Have you seen that? Doesn't it drive you crazy?* The display shows all of these options, like 20% and 30%. I asked, 'Where's the just give me a freakin' burrito and don't spit in it' option?"

The rewritten joke is tighter, recent, and has a more robust punchline. I wrote two "toppers" that expanded upon the original joke. We aimed to write and deliver a page and a half of the material at graduation. Eventually, I ended up with fifteen jokes to tell over four minutes.

Before sharing my thoughts on how the routine went, I'd like to pass along six brief insights I gained from the Comedy Workshoppe experience.

Feedback. Jeff told us that he wouldn't let us fail if we worked hard and gracefully accepted feedback. He and his team would rewrite jokes to shorten set-ups or strengthen punch lines. I always wanted to soak in the feedback provided by a professional comedian, someone who's been there and done that. After all, I did pay $600 to participate in the workshop. Also, I observed that many people don't accept feedback gracefully or ignore it altogether. Many became defensive and argued with Jeff when he offered suggestions on how to improve. You can imagine how their turn at the mic went.

Delivery. Comedy is 90 percent delivery, just like any other presentation. I've made thousands of presentations over my lifetime; dare I say, 10,000. I can easily throw up some PowerPoint slides on a screen and discuss the key points. But a stand-up comedy routine isn't a presentation. Delivering a routine is more like acting. You've got to remember your lines, *how* to say your lines, and *when* to say your lines. It takes significantly more brainpower to remember the set, from the opening joke to the closing callback. I've often said, "Practice breeds confidence." So, I practiced over fifty times while on walks, working out, in front of my ever-patient wife, driving, shopping, and almost anywhere.

Imperfection. My performance is far from perfect. Even with all the practice, I stumbled through some of my lines and lost my place sometimes. Why? I'd never experienced an audience laughing at my original material or the distractions in a comedy club—staff taking orders and serving drinks, for example. After spending a lifetime trying to be perfect in front of others, I began to display some vulnerabilities. In the imperfections, I found myself connecting with the audience. I wasn't polished, but I was relatable. I let my guard down and enjoyed being on stage, sharing some of my humorous takes and connecting with the audience.

Let 'em laugh. Jeff hammered me during practice because I always talked over the audience's laughter. During practice, I'd move to the next joke, more concerned about delivering the content than connecting with the audience. Jeff told me, "If they laugh, enjoy the moment. If they keep laughing, enjoy the moment as long as they do." That's the goal, after all.

Encouragement. One of my fellow participants, Jason, took the workshop to challenge himself. During the first session, he told us that public speaking terrified him. Like Jerry Seinfeld said, "People would rather be in the casket than deliver the eulogy." But Jason's stuff was hilarious. After watching him struggle on stage a couple of times, I offered words of encouragement. I told him that his content was fantastic. Encouragement is oxygen to the soul. Because he embraced the process, I watched Jason gain confidence and ultimately deliver a hilarious graduation routine. After graduation, he thanked me for the encouragement I had given him.

Stretch. John Maxwell's Law of the Rubber Band states, "True life begins at the end of our comfort zone, and we arrive there by stretching."[41] I wanted to enlarge my comfort zone to become a more effective speaker and writer. My wife, Carla, will tell you that there were many nights I came home from the workshop frustrated. I struggled with self-confidence. I haven't been pushed like that in years.

Back to The Punchline. I wrote four minutes' worth of material, but was on stage for approximately seven minutes. Why? A couple of reasons: I forgot some of my lines, and let 'em laugh. I blinked, and it was over.

I got to stand on the stage where famous comedians performed, from Richard Pryor to Robin Williams, Chris Rock to Jerry Seinfeld. The fear never went away, but I stepped up to the microphone anyway. That's courage. What a terrifying, humbling, and satisfying experience!

Stepping into the comedy spotlight wasn't about the jokes themselves—it was about how I faced my fears, embraced vulnerability, and leaned into the discomfort of potential failure. Courage isn't just about the big leaps but how you prepare, how you recover when things don't go as planned, and how you use those moments to grow.

I apply what I learned in training, speaking engagements, and consulting to this day, helping everyone I meet find the courage to explore their potential. And if a few people laugh along the way, that's a bonus.

THE HARDEST BATTLE YOU'LL EVER FIGHT

I was bullied during my adolescent years, and I have shared my story several times in support of National Bullying Prevention Week. After one of the first times I shared my story, I received stinging criticism that I bullied others, and my attitudes, words, and actions toward them were hurtful. Just as I was shaped by my bullying experience, I now understand that those I bullied were impacted by my behavior toward them.

The psychological term for my behavior is "Displacement—a defense mechanism in which a person redirects a negative emotion from its original source to a less threatening recipient."[42] In my anger, frustration, fear, and anxiety, I have no doubt that I took my negative emotions out on others. Unfortunately, my regretful behavior continued into my college and early career. I became the intimidator out of fear of being intimidated.

I accept responsibility for my conduct, and if you were ever the brunt of my regretful behavior, please forgive me. It wasn't until the Lord got hold of me that I put down my defenses. I discovered what it meant to love people...

"Love is patient and kind; love does not envy or boast; it is not arrogant or rude. It does not insist on its own way; it is not irritable or resentful; it does not rejoice at wrongdoing but rejoices with the truth. Love bears all things, believes all things, hopes all things, endures all things. Love never ends." (1 Corinthians 13:4-8, English Standard Version)

Admittedly, I'm still a work in progress and have a long, long way to go. How about you? If you're a bully or intimidate others, you may be displacing your emotions on others. Here's more of my story.

After becoming a Christian in the eighth grade, I shared my newfound faith with everyone. I hoped my relationship with Jesus would be contagious. After a few months of sharing, multiple friends called and asked to come to church with me. I was so excited! Some came and responded to the good news as I had. But others decided that the Christian faith wasn't for them. These friends who'd rejected the message began to reject me as well.

Being bullied became a constant pattern in my life. I was ridiculed and ostracized; I was physically or verbally threatened on several occasions because of my beliefs. One semester in high school, a group of tough guys began intimidating me. They'd sneak up on me and whisper, "Do you want to fight? You'd better watch yourself after school. We're gonna kick your butt!" They were relentless. The bullies stared and laughed at me in class, followed me down the halls every day, and prevented me from getting into my locker. I was scared to death and felt like no one could help me. But even in the face of fear, it took courage to keep showing up each day. Like John Wayne said, "Courage is being scared to death but saddling up anyway. "

But I didn't know how to fight back. I was a scrawny, five-foot-two kid who weighed eighty pounds soaking wet. The bullies seemed like they were ten feet tall. Their intimidation became overbearing, so I went to see the school counselor. After hearing my story, he began escorting me to the bike rack after school for the next month. I'd unlock my bike, hop on, and ride like the wind, hoping to get home before the bullies caught me.

One time, I was home alone, and the doorbell rang. Two bullies were at the door. They tried to pull me outside and beat me up—in a nice, middle-class neighborhood, no less! I forced the door shut. They looked for another way into the house, calling me names as I hid inside. I tried to call my neighbors for help. No one was home. I was so scared that the bullies would find a way into my house that I called the police. The bullies left.

My dad came home, and I told him what had happened. Trying to help me, he called the bullies' parents and had stern conversations with them. Well, you can imagine how the bullies reacted. Their threats, intimidation, and pressure grew worse. During P.E. the next day, the bullies told me I'd pay for my dad's calls.

Somehow, I managed to hold onto my faith and pray for God's protection throughout it all. I trusted God's promise in Isaiah 41:10: "Fear not, for I am with you; be not dismayed, for I am your God; I will strengthen you, I will help you, I will uphold you with my righteous right hand" (ESV).

I surrounded myself with other believers and found support. I was never physically harmed, but I was emotionally scarred. Being bullied was humiliating and embarrassing. Admittedly, I've struggled with resentment toward those bullies and wanted to get revenge over the years. It took a long time for me to forgive them and overcome my fear and anger. On one side, they taught me to trust God and persevere. On the other side, I learned how to hide my faith and my heart from others as a form of self-protection.

Eventually, I grew out of the five-foot-two frame into a six-foot-one frame. I matured physically, emotionally, and spiritually. However, it wasn't my physical changes that made the difference; it was the courage to forgive, let go of resentment, and choose growth over bitterness. My confidence grew more potent, and bullies no longer intimidated me. I stick up for myself. But when I sense someone is trying to threaten me or someone else, I have a visceral reaction (i.e., hair standing up on the back of my neck) that motivates me to stand up for myself and others.

Statistics show that 20 percent of children ages 12 to 18 years old experience some type of bullying – unwanted, aggressive behavior meant to hurt.[43] As you might know firsthand, bullying often graduates from playgrounds to workplaces. How do you prevent and reduce bullying? It can be complex. But based on my experience, I recommend the following seven ways:

- *Keep the faith*. I ran to God and sought His help in my time of need. He heard my cries and protected me. My faith in Him grew more profound because of my experience.
- *Speak up*. If you are being bullied, tell someone – a teacher, an adult, a parent, a friend, a counselor, or anyone you trust. Don't feel embarrassed; ask for help. It took me a long time to tell anyone that I was being bullied. Finally, I told my parents and teachers. Perhaps it wouldn't have lasted as long or been as intense if I'd told someone earlier.
- *Surround yourself*. Seek support, safety, and solace with your friends and family. I leaned into my church youth group and will never forget their encouragement.
- *Stick up for yourself*. Sometimes, you have to dig deep and find the courage to overcome your fear. Let the bully know

you're no longer going to put up with it. I'm not encouraging violence. I am encouraging a resolve deep within that prevents anyone from unwanted aggressive behavior. Tell the bully to stop.
- *Be someone's hero.* Don't stand on the sidelines if you see someone being bullied. If someone says something, stand up for the bullied person; if you see something, speak up. I wish I had more heroes willing to stand up for me. Now, I try to be someone's hero.
- *Create awareness and a culture of safety.* Teachers, administrators, parents, and students can all play a crucial role in preventing bullying. Educate everyone on what bullying is and isn't. Teach respect, dignity, and what to do if someone is being bullied. Listen. Be empathetic. Protect others.
- *Forgive and forget.* It took me a long time to resolve my anger and resentment. I learned that it's not good to hold onto grudges. If you do, you become bitter.

It's not just about what happens to you, but how you respond that builds your character. It took courage to face my pain, let go of my bitterness, and forgive—not just the bullies but myself. Through self-reflection and change, I realized the how—how I chose to deal with my past—was far more important than the bullying itself. This journey taught me the value of humility, empathy, and the power of change, reminding us that true leadership and growth are revealed in how we act and treat others.

COURAGE OVER COMFORT: THE LEADERSHIP CHOICE

In both the comedy club and the bullying experiences, courage wasn't about eliminating fear or avoiding discomfort—it was about how I chose to face those challenges. It's not the absence of fear that defines leaders; it's how we push through it. And courage is not "fake it till you make it," either. True courage owns vulnerability, imperfection, and, ultimately, change. There will always be wolves, but we can face them, even dance with them, and win.

PRINCIPLE
Own your fears; never let them own you

QUESTIONS

How do you typically respond to fear, and how could changing your approach to fear help you grow as a leader?

_____
_____
_____

What is one fear or challenge in your life that you've been avoiding? What small steps can you take to start facing it today?

_____
_____
_____

Think about a time when you allowed fear to hold you back. What might have been different if you had focused on how you faced the challenge instead of just the fear itself?

_____
_____
_____

CHAPTER 8

Do You Believe?

"I always wanted to be somebody,
but now I realize I should have been more specific."
— LILLY TOMLIN

Imagine a world where Luke Skywalker didn't become a Jedi Knight, fight galactic battles, destroy the Death Star, and defeat the Evil Empire. Instead, he retreated to his home planet, Tatooine, became a scavenger, and sold used hovercrafts across the galaxy. The movie would be called *Car Wars*.

What if Daniel-son never found the courage to stand up to his bullies, ignored Miyagi, and eventually got waxed off? The movie would be renamed *"The Coward Kid."*

Or, if Coaches Boone and Yost couldn't overcome their prejudices, the high school football team remained dysfunctional, and finished last in their conference? The movie would be entitled *"No One Remembers the Titans."*

But these aren't the stories we know. Young Luke was mentored by Obi-Wan Kenobi and Yoda, learning how to use his lightsaber, connect with the Force, and helped overcome the Evil Empire in *Star Wars*. Daniel-son was mentored by Miyagi, learned to confront his fears, and overcame the bullies in the *Karate Kid*. And everyone *remembers the Titans* because the team prevailed over prejudice, practiced hard, and won the state football championship.

What's one of the common threads among the stories? The characters weren't heroes when they started, but they all had untapped potential. What is potential? It's the capacity of raw talent and the qualities that make one successful or valuable in the future. To realize their potential (convert possibility into potency), those heroes went on a journey of transformation.

POTENTIAL WASTED IS POTENTIAL LOST

How would you like to be a hero in your own story, personally or professionally? Would you like to grow stronger, have a greater influence on your world, and make a positive impact? I bet you do. All you need to do is develop your potential. But here's the bad news. It takes hard work. Most people don't actively pursue becoming the person they were created to be. Why? You know the typical excuses: not enough time, other priorities, no resources or support.

Composer Gian Carlo Menotti forcefully stated, "Hell begins on that day when God grants us a clear vision of all that we might have achieved, of all the gifts we wasted, of all that we might have done that we did not do. Unrealized potential is a tragic waste."[44]

What if you embarked on a development journey? If you reached your potential, what might it look like? What would it mean to you, personally and professionally? How would you and those around you benefit? What if you don't?

Here's some good news. Just like the heroes in my favorite movies, we don't have to find the path to growth; it finds us. In fact, you're on it right now, whether you know it or not, and whether you like it or not.

OUT OF MY LEAGUE AND ONTO THE LEADERBOARD

With his icy blue eyes, Chris stared at me for a moment and then said with an exasperated tone, "I'm not interested. You're wasting your time and mine. As a matter of fact, you don't need to come back, ever again."

He was right, I was wasting his time. I'd visited his store frequently to make a case on why he needed to carry the new product line I represented. I thought enthusiasm and persistence would eventually pay off, and Chris would become a new customer. But I couldn't close the deal. As a matter of fact, I wasn't closing any deals.

Ralston Purina hired me to launch a new premium pet food named Pro Plan—competition for market leaders, such as Science Diet and Iams. A friend referred me to Paul, the hiring manager in charge of forming the Southeast sales team. After our interview (and lack of candidates in the Alabama/Mississippi market), Paul decided to give me a chance, even though I had absolutely no selling experience. When Paul called to offer the job to me, he made it clear that he was "hiring *potential*" and that we'd see how it would go. Not a resounding vote of confidence, but I decided to accept the role anyway. Why? I wanted to make a career change, and the offer was too good to turn down. It included a 30% pay raise, a substantial bonus, comprehensive benefits, and a company car – a sweet deal for someone without the necessary experience.

Right before I started the role, Paul called and said he was sending some brochures to learn about the Pro Plan product line and a list of pet and feed store accounts in my new territory. Since Paul was setting up a new sales team and he couldn't spend much time with me, he suggested that I read a few books on selling, pick my favorite principles, and apply them. He also told me that enthusiasm and persistence would win over any customer. Lastly, he said it was time to hit the road and begin selling Pro Plan. "Call me if you have any questions, Preston!"

Using the account list, I mapped out my route and hit the road. I began with the larger cities, such as Birmingham and Jackson, by contacting local pet and feed store owners. Then, I visited rural markets. If you've never driven in the rural Southeast, there are long stretches of two-lane roads with only farmland and cows in sight. This is when I developed my affection for country music, as it was typically the only music my radio would pick up.

I went from town to town, from pet store to pet store, and from feed store to feed store. I discovered that a few accounts had already picked up Pro Plan, but the vast majority hadn't. Why? Due to Purina's dominant market share in the grocery channel, many store owners considered Purina a competitor—even an enemy. When customers purchased their pet food in a grocery store, they were less likely to visit and buy from a pet or feed store. To many pet and feed store owners, the idea of carrying a Ralston product just wasn't palatable.

After my initial two-month swing across Alabama and Mississippi, I attended a Pro Plan sales meeting at Purina's headquarters in St. Louis. The marketing team introduced a Pro Plan line extension called "Turkey and Barley." Part of the product knowledge was a kibble tasting. Yes, a kibble tasting. I'll never forget the moment. Teams gathered at designated tables to review the packaging, ingredients, and product differentiation. Then the moment of truth. Paul asked his new team, "You wouldn't feed something to your dog that you couldn't feed yourself, would you?" We all looked at each other with a sense of disbelief. I shrugged my shoulders and thought, *when in Rome...* Thankfully, I managed to hide my angst, not embarrass myself, and comply with the culture. *That's a gooood boy, Preston!*

I soon returned to my market and began calling on store owners again. Most of my focus was on cold calling for new business development. However, I soon discovered that my efforts weren't yielding the desired results. I had great conversations with store owners, but I hadn't closed any deals. Reports from the company showed that I was in last place for the number of opened accounts and the percentage change in volume. I was hired for my potential, but as Bear Bryant used to say, "Potential just means you aren't worth a sh** yet." To reach my potential and not let down the hiring manager who took a risk on me, I decided I needed some sales training. But I didn't know where to start.

The last straw happened at The Pet Stop in Vestavia, Alabama. The owner's name was Chris. His store was located in a neighborhood near my house, making it easy for me to visit regularly. Chris was a big *supporter of Science Diet* and *Iams*. As I got to know Chris, I discovered that he was fervently resentful toward Purina because the company's marketing drew traffic and potential sales away from his store. During every visit, I showed him the informative brochures and explained Pro Plan's latest marketing campaign. But I couldn't gain his commitment. He shared his gripes: no space, no money, happy with competitors, not wanting to support "the competition." One day, Chris told me, "I'm not interested. You're wasting your time and mine. As a matter of fact, you don't need to come back ever again."

After a series of similar events at other stores, I approached Paul and told him that I didn't think I was suited for the role, and that he probably made a mistake in hiring me. He probed with a few questions and seemed empathetic. He asked me to walk him through my "selling" approach. Right away, he concluded that I didn't follow a process. For example, there were no opening statements, probing for needs, handling objections, or closing techniques. He wasn't sure what to do because Purina didn't offer a formal sales training program, since they typically hired experienced sales representatives. But he had an idea. "What if you took an external sales training course?" He charged me with finding some options, and once we picked the best one, he'd find the funds to pay for it.

How Training Turned the Tables

I conducted research and found a course offered by a fairly well-known company named Dale Carnegie Training. Have you heard of it? Dale Carnegie is best known for writing the classic book *"How to Win Friends and Influence People,"* and his namesake training organization offered a human relations-oriented sales training course. But the fee and time commitment seemed outrageous: $1,000 for a twelve-week course that met one night a week for three hours, loads of homework, and on-the-job application. It would take a gigantic commitment on my part to complete the course, but I was willing to do anything to improve my status as the worst sales rep on Paul's team.

Not only was I disappointed by my sales results, but I'd also become depressed. I'd lost confidence and was fearful of losing my job. Even my outward appearance reflected my low spirits. Then, I met Joe.

Joe was the owner of the local Dale Carnegie franchise and sales course facilitator. I came to learn that he was formerly the top Dale Carnegie salesperson in the world, a former PGA Tour member, and a local radio show host. I was impressed. And for some reason, he took an interest in me.

Everything Joe taught was eye-opening: How to open a sales call (e.g., "If there were a way to increase your sales by $X, you'd want to know about it, wouldn't you?"), how to ask probing questions, listening skills, the difference between features and benefits, providing a value proposition, how to smoke out and overcome objections, and closing techniques.

The course's methodology was to teach a selling principle in the classroom, apply it on the job, and then return the following week to share the results. Joe coached the participants as we practiced the principles. Many times, we failed, but that's where the learning happened. As time passed, I applied the principles, and they worked.

My confidence started to grow. I began fearlessly opening sales calls – gaining a store owner's undivided attention, listening for customer needs, demonstrating how Pro Plan would benefit their business, overcoming objections, and most of all, closing sales.

I had more pep in my step, and my outward appearance began to reflect how I felt on the inside. I even started attending class wearing a sports coat, dress slacks, and a button-down shirt. My newfound confidence shone, and people took notice.

Over the twelve-week course, class members participated in a "Sales Talk" competition, where each member took turns pitching their product or service and applying the new skills they'd learned. When it was my turn in the first round, I passionately demonstrated how I'd grown and pitched Pro Plan, utilizing all the key selling principles and techniques. Surprisingly, my peers voted me into the finals. But Monte, a professional salesperson, future CEO, and community leader, was a formidable competitor.

To differentiate myself and take home the trophy, I decided that the key to winning would be showmanship—demonstrating Pro Plan's real-life effect. No, I wasn't going to ask everyone to taste a kibble. However, my idea did involve a dog. I was hesitant to execute the concept, but during my preparation, I remembered a quote from Dale Carnegie's *"How to Stop Worrying and Start Living."* It reads, "I cannot write a work commiserate with Shakespeare, but I can write a book by me." The quote inspired me with the confidence to become a first-rate Preston Poore, not a second-rate someone else. To take a chance and differentiate myself from the competition.

The big day came, and Monte went first. He gave a passionate and convincing talk about construction and business development in his new pitch for multi-million-dollar real estate development. Smooth. Impressive. Surely, he would win. But that didn't stop me from trying.

I rose to present in my chalk-striped, gray suit, tie, and polished shoes. I had a conversation with the audience, as if I were speaking directly to a store owner. After walking through my opening statement, asking questions, fleshing out and overcoming objections, it was time for the close.

I told the audience that there was no better way to believe what I was telling them about the health benefits of Pro Plan than to show them a living example. To the audience's surprise, my wife, Carla, appeared at the back of the room, holding our Dachshund, Sally. I introduced Carla and Sally. Sally's tail wagged as she recognized me. Carla put Sally down, and Sally immediately ran across the room to me. The class cheered and roared with laughter, enjoying the pleasant surprise appearance. "The proof is in the pudding! Sally has been eating Pro Plan for the last year. Her coat shines, her energy level is high, and she is healthier than when we fed her grocery store brand pet food."

"Who wouldn't want their pet to look and feel like Sally? All it takes is offering Pro Plan to your customers." To close, I asked, "Would you like to place the large or medium-sized rack with your first 500-pound order?"

No one in the class placed an order, but I did receive rousing applause. Come to think of it, they may have been cheering for Sally.

Regardless, it was time to vote. Joe counted the ballots and announced, "You've selected Preston as our 'Sales Talk Champion.' Congratulations Preston!" I proudly received a plaque that I still treasure to this day.

Even more rewarding was the fact that I eventually became one of the top Pro Plan representatives in the Southeast. I grew, and my company grew as well. All because someone believed in me, made a way for me, and coached me.

What about Chris?

After completing the Dale Carnegie Sales Course, I gathered the strength to revisit Chris, even though he had told me not to come back. When I walked into the store, he seemed surprised to see me. "What can I do for you today? Would you like to buy some Science Diet?" he asked with a friendly grin. I chuckled and smiled back.

"If there was a way for you to make an incremental $500 per month, you'd want to know about it wouldn't you?"

"Yes, I would. Sales have been a little slow over the past few months."

I walked him through how Pro Plan could help him and the marketing campaign Ralston developed to drive traffic to the pet store.

Chris showed interest, so I went for the close. "Would you like to place the large or medium sized rack with your first 500-pound order?"

Then I was silent. The Dale Carnegie Course taught me to stop selling when you move to the closing step. It can be awkward, but the first one to speak typically concedes. If I spoke first, I would lose the sale. If Chris spoke first, he'd either say "yes," "no," or provide another objection. My training taught me that all of this was part of the selling process.

We stood face-to-face in the corner of the store, surrounded by the sounds of dogs barking, birds chirping, and shoppers walking up and down the aisles. It became awkward. I reminded myself to let him speak first. Self-control was key.

After what seemed like an eternity, Chris said, "Yes. Where do I sign?"

After we completed the paperwork, I asked, "At one point, you told me I was wasting my time and not to come back. But you placed an order today. What was the difference between today and all of the other times we talked?"

"You asked for the order." he said.

GROWTH AIN'T ACCIDENTAL: MAKE IT COUNT

Faced with the options of success or failure, winning or losing, continuing or quitting, I chose to change. I decided that the only way to succeed, win, and continue was to stretch. Here are some steps to stretch to your potential.

Define Your Gap. When I began engaging potential customers about Pro Plan, I quickly realized that I couldn't sell. The results spoke loud and clear. My natural abilities, enthusiasm, and persistence, while important, weren't enough. I needed to learn a new skill. Failure wasn't an option. I had a young family depending on me, friends who referred me, and a manager who took a chance on me. I could either face my gap or face the consequences.

Be Deliberate. What's the difference between growth and stagnation? *You.* You won't develop accidentally. You must carefully determine *how* you will close your gaps. Make the time and be willing to pay the price. Do everything in your power to secure the support, funding, and time you need to develop the skill. I took the initiative after identifying my selling gap. I approached Paul, my manager, with my need and gained his support. He secured the $1,000 fee for the Dale Carnegie Sales Course and allowed me to adjust my schedule to attend the training. Once enrolled, I wholeheartedly committed to attending the classes, doing the homework, applying the principles, and sharing my learnings every week for three months.

Apply, Apply, Apply. It's been said that knowledge is power. In truth, the *application* of knowledge is power. You need to put what you learned into practice; turn thoughts and words into action.

Knowledge must inform and shape our actions. The fuel of development is application, nothing more, nothing less.

Self-Reflect. Once you've applied the acquired knowledge, it's time to reflect – think deeply about your experience. What worked well? What were your successes? How did you see your strengths come to life, and how will you build upon them? What didn't go well? Did you fail? That's okay—what did you learn? What adjustments do you need to make? What limiting self-beliefs are holding me back? I recommend keeping a journal to record your thoughts. If you journal over several months, you'll be able to revisit your reflections and see the progress you've made.

Be Accountable. To achieve the results you desire, it's beneficial to have a coach, manager, peer, or friend ask probing questions, offer advice, and provide encouragement. Connect with someone you trust and share your plan with them. Similar to the above self-reflection questions, empower your accountability partner to ask questions like:
- Wins: What's going well? What are you most proud of? What did you learn? How will you replicate or build upon it?
- Challenges: What's not going well? Why? What did you learn? How will you course correct?
- Goals: What do you want to accomplish moving forward? By when? How do you define success? Do you anticipate any challenges? How will you overcome them?
- Support: How can I help you?

True growth is not just about what you achieve but *how* you get there. In pursuing growth with intention, you don't just elevate yourself—you create a ripple effect that touches everyone around you. That's the power of turning potential into potency.

IS THAT ALL YOU'VE GOT?

"Dammit! I don't get this guy," I yelled as I slammed the door, and wondered out loud to my wife if I'd made a bad career decision.

I'd changed companies and took a new opportunity to get us closer to home, relocating from Hershey, Pennsylvania, to Montgomery, Alabama. It was a homecoming of sorts. Carla and I met and married in Birmingham; our children were born at St. Vincent's Hospital, and many of our family members still resided in the area.

I moved out of a successful sales and marketing role with Hershey into a "franchise leadership" position with The Coca-Cola Company. My new role required me to represent The Company's interests to the local bottling partner, develop plans, gain strategic alignment, and help deliver results. I felt a little over my ski tips: a new role, a new market, a new industry, and new people. I knew it would take every bit of my shaky leadership, communication, sales, and marketing skills to succeed.

Why? My primary contact, Rick, had a reputation as a driven leader who was very demanding and challenging to get along with. He was a towering man with a commanding presence and an intensity that made him seem larger than life—someone you wouldn't want to cross in a boardroom or on the football field. He'd recently been appointed as Market Unit VP and tasked with turning a very low-performing operation around.

I'll never forget my first presentation to Rick and his team. He asked me to put together a marketing plan for a local university. I thought it would be a piece of cake based on my experience at Hershey. I invested two weeks pulling together detailed plans and felt good about what I developed. I presented my plan during his monthly operating meeting in front of his key leaders. After I finished, I asked Rick, "What do you think?"

Rick paused and asked, "Is that all you've got?"

There was a long, awkward silence in the room. I squeaked out a "Yes."

"I'm expecting more," Rick replied. "Your plan is very disappointing. Go back to the drawing board and bring back something that will help us win in the market."

This wasn't the first time that I'd stumbled with Rick by not delivering on expectations. As I sat simmering, I thought to myself, *I'm never going to gain credibility in Rick's eyes. I don't know what to do.*

Fast forward a few months. I'd been working hard to gain Rick's trust and respect, but with little to show for it. Then, one day, after a market execution tour, we were leaning against a grocery store checkout lane conveyor belt, recapping the day.

After summarizing the sub-par execution, I changed the subject and said to Rick, "I know my work hasn't lived up to your expectations. I am working hard to get better and am on a steep learning curve. I'm positive that I have what it takes and can help you turn the business around."

Rick just looked at me.

I continued, "If you'll take me under your wing and teach me everything you know, I will learn and do everything it takes to help you, and the team, win."

Another long, awkward pause… I think he liked the pauses.

"Preston, I've been hard on you, testing you, to see if you have what it takes. You know what? I think you do, and I know you can help me. I'll take you up on your offer."

Rick began including me in all of his market visits and key leadership meetings. We collaboratively developed robust plans, focused the team on the work that mattered, and executed with excellence. The Market Unit gained positive momentum and began to receive national recognition. Based on our strong performance, we were privileged to pilot new brands and packages before their national launches (e.g., Fridge Pack and Diet Coke with Lemon; more on the hits and misses of these and other product launches in Chapter 10). We also re-negotiated key marketing asset contracts in the face of fierce competition. Lastly, we became a model team, importing and exporting talent. Under Rick's tremendous leadership, *we* achieved a significant victory.

But when I think about Rick, I don't think about our accomplishments. I remember the friendship we developed over the years. I remember all of the windshield time we had together, driving from town to town, sales center to sales center. Under Rick's sometimes-rough exterior, I discovered a genuine person who really cared about people. Rick and I found that we shared many values, including our faith, during our many conversations. I'll never forget the countless belly laughs we had together, the confidence he placed in me, and how he took me under his wing.

Rick and I still stay in touch and talk occasionally. Recently, I heard he was retiring, so I called him to check in. He said a twenty-eight-year career with Coke and seven years in the NFL were enough. "It is time," he said. The towering, "intimidating" man I mentioned earlier played professional football during his first career and won a Super Bowl championship with the Washington Redskins—beating my beloved Denver Broncos, nonetheless. Rick is a winner in whatever he does. More importantly, he's a leader.

Rick, thank you for being who you are, mentoring me, and leading well. You've made a positive difference and left a great legacy.

Do you have a mentor in your life? If not, I recommend that you find one and ask them for help. On the other side of the coin, are you a mentor to someone? If not, consider mentoring someone. If you do, you'll make a positive difference as Rick did with me.

THE BELIEF ELEVATION PYRAMID

What is it that separates those who get by from those who soar? Reflecting on my time with Rick, it wasn't just his coaching that shaped me – it was the belief he instilled in me as he coached. The how of our growth, just like the how of our leadership, starts with belief. Not just belief in ourselves, but belief in a greater thing – belief in others and our potential impact.

It provides the core beliefs on which the Belief Elevation Pyramid is built, and which propels potential into 'the field' of true performance.

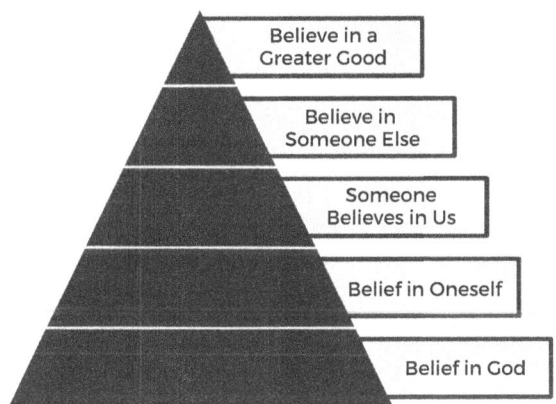

Belief in God. Gives you a sense of morality, hope, and resolve to overcome hardships. It can give you something about who you are and why you are here that is not simply your set of life goals. It can provide a kind of mental and emotional resilience; it has been linked to higher levels of psychological well-being, coping, and quality of life.

Belief in Oneself. Self-belief is fundamental to success in life and at work. It is correlated with what psychologists call self-efficacy, or belief in your capabilities to accomplish goals. High self-efficacy is associated with the establishment of higher goals, more motivation, greater resistance to setbacks, and ultimately greater success.

Someone Believes in Us. Having a coach, mentor, or supporter who believes in us provides us with an increased sense of self-esteem, encourages risk-taking behaviors, and supports resilience. Being believed in by others can be the boost we need to work towards and achieve what we thought was impossible.

Believe in Someone Else. Leading by backing other people is a critical leadership behavior. Believing in others fosters trust and teamwork, while also enhancing morale and productivity.

Believe in a Greater Good. Believing in playing a role in or contributing to something larger than oneself is a key ingredient of personal and professional fulfillment, including for leaders. This belief often operates in tandem with beliefs about purpose, legacy, and impact, but has a longer-term dimension of making a meaningful difference in the world.

WHEN EXCELLENCE TAKES CENTER STAGE

There we were, sitting in the front row of the Bolshoi Theater in Moscow. A place I never imagined we'd be in a million years. Built in 1825, the theater is the centerpiece of Russian culture and artistry.

In 2019, I was invited to lead a two-day workshop for executive leaders from Coca-Cola Hellenic and The Coca-Cola Company. One of the leaders gifted Carla and me two tickets to Swan Lake, the renowned classical ballet set to Tchaikovsky's famous score. We were literally in the front row next to the aisle. The only thing in front of us was a short barrier, and then the orchestra. But my mind was far away from the ballet.

I was focused on the next day's workshop and the high expectations of bringing twenty key leaders to Moscow. And truthfully, ballet isn't my cup of tea. I prefer action to art, football to dancing. But when in Moscow, do as the Muscovites do.

I couldn't help but notice the theater's opulence and the Russian murmuring all around us. I felt like a Connecticut Yankee in King Arthur's court. What hit me was unexpected. The lights dimmed, and with the first dance step, I was amazed at the ballet dancers' athleticism; they ran and effortlessly leaped like gazelles. And the music was breathtaking. My ambivalence turned to awe.

During Act Three, I noticed the first-chair violinist, Lev Klychkov, with his long mane, stand at the conductor's prompting. I was distracted by Klychkov's visible nerves, blinking eyes, sweat dripping down his forehead, and a twitch in his arm. The audience's fixed gazes filled the air with palpable tension. All of a sudden, he closed his eyes, reopened them, and wham! He began his solo with a collective release as his music filled the air.

Klychkov played with stylish expressiveness and emotional depth that mesmerized me. In a moment of deep concentration and surrender to the music, the violin soared. Even though Klychkov was so immersed in his performance and seemed oblivious to the outside world, he captivated the audience with his passion and technical precision. When Klychkov's solo concluded, he took his seat with a sublime look of satisfaction.

At the end of Swan Lake, the audience rose to a standing ovation as people rushed the stage to cheer and throw roses, expressing their love and appreciation for the performers' talent and hard work.

I didn't throw any roses, but my perception and appreciation of the arts transformed that night. Believe it or not, I listen to Tchaikovsky's masterpiece from time to time. And I'll never forget Klychkov's nerves preceding an excellent and riveting performance—a virtuoso in the flow.

What does this have to do with leadership and personal growth? Only when we are in our flow, the state of total absorption and engagement, and using our skills at the highest level, do we grow into our potential. It's when you feel most alive and where your work is more than work; it's a form of expressing your God-given talents, skills, and abilities. Eric Liddle, Olympic champion, once said, "I believe God made me for a purpose. But he made me fast. And when I run, I feel his pleasure." When Liddle ran, he was in the flow.

As a leader, you reach your peak potential by finding your flow in your role—aligning your skills with your tasks so seamlessly that you achieve exceptional results and inspire those around you. It's not just about reaching your potential but also about how you get there.

Potential alone isn't enough—it's how you choose to develop it that creates standing ovations and transformation.

PRINCIPLE
Develop with intention—both in yourself and others

QUESTIONS

What steps can you take today to unlock your untapped potential, both personally and professionally?

_____

_____

_____

Who in your life can mentor you or help you grow, and how can you actively seek their guidance?

_____

_____

_____

How can you apply what you've learned about your potential to inspire growth in those around you?

_____

_____

_____

CHAPTER 9

Cutting Through the Noise

*"I love deadlines.
I like the whooshing sound they make as they fly by."*
—DOUGLAS ADAMS

Ever feel like you're drowning in decisions and tasks? Trust me, I've been there.

Fortune 500 managers waste approximately 530,000 days making decisions, potentially squandering $250 million in annual wages.[45] The average worker spends 51% of every workday on low- to no-value tasks.[46]

Solvable? Yes, but it takes work.

The key to developing as a leader isn't just about hard work—it's about mastering decision-making and prioritization. These two skills can transform chaos into clarity for you and your team. It's not about what tasks we tackle; it's about *how* we prioritize, approach, and execute them.

SNOWED UNDER, LESSONS LEARNED

January 29, 2014: First journal entry of the new year. I am thankful and full of joy this morning. I survived Atlanta's "Snowpocalypse" yesterday. Here's my story.

The National Weather Service issued a winter storm warning for the Atlanta Metro area on Monday, January 27, predicting one to two inches of snow for the next day. Nothing freaks Atlantans out more than a good snowstorm. It can cripple the city. Why? The "city in a forest" has deep tree coverage and rolling hills. The above-ground power lines become vulnerable to falling trees, which are weighed down by snow. Power can be lost for days. At the threat of snow, we panic and rush to buy bread, milk, and alcohol to endure the event, as if it were the end of the world.

Some would argue that Atlantans don't know how to drive in good weather, so you can imagine how a few snowflakes transform our streets into a giant bumper-car ride. The city government lacked sufficient snowplows to clear major thoroughfares, neglected to salt the streets, and failed to encourage residents to stay off the roads. Leadership was absent and didn't take the forecast seriously. In fact, the governor and mayor were attending a luncheon where the mayor was honored as the Associated Press's "Georgian of the Year." The mayor overconfidently tweeted, "Atlanta, we are ready for the snow."

We weren't.

I was overconfident, too. I grew up in Colorado and didn't really understand all the fuss. While I was confident that the imminent storm posed no personal threat, I sent a note to my team instructing them to keep an eye on the weather and leave early if necessary.

I drove to work as usual on Tuesday, a 60-minute, 18-mile commute. During a noon meeting, I looked out the 16th-floor conference room window and saw giant snowflakes. The wind was picking up, and the storm intensified into what would ultimately become whiteout conditions. I looked down at the streets below and noticed that the intersections around the building were already jammed with traffic. My friend Jennifer called and encouraged me to leave the office. She warned me that any delay might mean I'd not make it home. I thought to myself, "Yeah, right. I'm from

Colorado. I can handle this. Y'all panic. I got this." I decided to ignore Jennifer's advice and finish the meeting.

My Noon meeting unexpectedly lasted until 1:45pm. The weather conditions deteriorated further, and traffic became snarled. From my vantage point on the 16th floor, I could see red taillights for miles. I gathered my belongings to begin my trek home. I raced down to the parking garage and noticed a long line of cars waiting to exit. I asked the security guard what was going on, and he told me that drivers on the street weren't allowing cars to exit the garage. It would take 90 minutes just to get out of the garage and onto the side street.

"How long has the parking garage been backed up?" I asked.

"About 45 minutes," he said. *Ugh.* If I'd ended the meeting at 1:00pm and gotten in my car, I might have avoided the mess. I turned around, returned to my office, and thought that if I waited a little longer, the traffic would dissipate. Boy, was I wrong.

I sat in my office for the next three hours, trying to decide whether to spend the night there or risk driving home. I decided to drive home and left at 4:45pm. It took an hour to go one mile. One of the smartest things I did before proceeding was to fill up my Toyota Camry's gas tank. The full tank gave me confidence that I wouldn't run out of gas as I made my way home. I packed water, a turkey sandwich, and vegetables. I also had an empty cup in case I needed to relieve myself. (*I know, sounds like I was preparing to trek across Alaska, not Atlanta, but that's the reality.*) I knew it would take an ample supply of patience and prayer to make it home safely.

And it did. My journey home took twelve hours to drive 18 miles. That's an average of 1.5 miles per hour. Driving was like playing "Frogger" (an old video game where the objective was to cross a river without getting caught by traps, hazards, and enemies). I literally dodged stalled, wrecked, or abandoned cars as I worked my way up I-75. It was difficult to start after coming to a complete stop while going uphill on ice.

After traveling ten miles in eleven hours, I began to cross the Chattahoochee bridge into Cobb County. Unlike the city of Atlanta, Cobb County cleared and treated the roads with salt. It took only thirty minutes to travel the eight remaining miles to my house. I arrived home at 4:30 am.

A blizzard of bad decisions
Schools and businesses all released their students at the same time. No salt was put on the roads. City leadership was asleep at the wheel. But I take personal responsibility for making a series of terrible decisions that led to my delay. I should have left at noon or stayed the night at the office. Not once did I pause to anticipate conditions or possible scenarios, let alone *pray* about what I should do.

Have you made one wrong decision that led to another, and the outcome wasn't what you planned? Leadership requires good choices, and the principles below can help.

- *Define the decision to be made.* This may be the hardest part. Write down the decision to be made or the problem to be solved. Why is it essential to make or solve? What if you don't decide or solve the problem? Is what you articulated the actual decision that needs to be made? How do you need to refine it?
- *Identify alternatives.* Brainstorm multiple options, gather relevant information, and engage those who need to be involved in the decision-making or problem-solving process. List the pros and cons of each alternative and predict possible outcomes. Ask questions like "Which option will produce the greatest results at the lowest cost?" "How

difficult will each choice be to implement?" "And are the alternatives congruent to key stakeholder's values?"
- *Choose the best alternative.* Evaluate each option and choose the one that will produce the highest return or good. Understand the risks you are taking, be able to explain how you made the decision, and move forward. A sage once told me, "A wise leader makes a decision and doesn't look back."
- *Implement your choice.* Develop a plan, secure the necessary resources, gain support, and implement your decision. Monitor its progress. Not all decisions result in positive outcomes. Some decisions are plain wrong. You'll make mistakes. If you make a wrong turn, get back on the highway.
- *Reflect on your choice and outcomes.* After the decision and implementation, take time to evaluate the results. What worked? What didn't work? What can I do differently next time? How can I apply what I learned? As Peter Drucker said, "Follow effective action with quiet reflection. From the quiet reflection will come even more effective action."
- *Be Tenacious.* Not long into my long drive home, I realized that I hadn't exercised sound judgment. But I still needed to get home. Thankfully, I didn't give up and stayed with it. When you've made a wrong decision or experienced a negative outcome, don't give up. Find the inner resolve, dogged persistence, and single-mindedness to keep moving forward. Meet your objective, complete the play, or finish the race. I am reminded of the following illustration about reaching the finish line despite adversity:

    Hours behind the runner in front of him, the last marathoner finally entered the Olympic stadium. By that time, the drama of the day's events was almost over, and most of the spectators had gone home. This athlete's story, however, was still playing out. Limping into the arena, the Tanzanian runner grimaced with every step, his knee bleeding and bandaged from an earlier fall. His ragged appearance immediately caught the attention of the remaining crowd, who cheered him on to the finish line.

Why did he stay in the race? What made him endure his injuries to the end? When asked these questions later, he replied, "My country did not send me 7,000 miles to start the race. They sent me 7,000 miles to finish it."[47]

- *Pray*. I've heard people say, "The only thing left to do is pray." But, despite my forgetfulness, praying is the first and most important thing I can do. Seek God for his protection, guidance, and wisdom. Ask him what to do, wait on him, and he will show you the way. Regarding my Snowpocalypse experience, I was way too confident in my winter driving experience. But when I got on the road, I quickly realized that it would take more than my driving skills to get home. I turned to God and asked for his help. Looking back, I am convinced beyond a doubt that the Lord protected me and enabled me to return home safely.

Snowpocalypse was a paralyzing weather event in the Atlanta Metro area. But the great thing about the city government is that people have learned from their mistakes. The next time snow and ice were forecasted, the city went into action mode. They announced school closures early, pre-treated the roads with over 3,000 tons of de-icing materials, and encouraged everyone to stay off the roads. Residents followed the leadership's direction, and Atlantans avoided the problems incurred during Snowpocalypse. I'd like to think I applied some hard-learned lessons myself.

The decisions we make in challenging situations are not just about what we do, but also about *how* we approach them. As leaders, embodying this philosophy enables us not only to reach our goals but also to do so in a way that inspires those around us. Remember, it's not just about starting the race; it's about finishing it with integrity and resilience.

TAMING THE URGENT BEAST

One of the most challenging roles of my career was on The Coca-Cola Company's Strategic Merchandising Team. For three years, I led a team responsible for developing retail point-of-sale displays and racks that enabled irresistible shopping experiences. The responsibilities included:

- 12 project managers and multiple cross-functional partners
- 10 suppliers
- ~$100M annual spend
- Tens of thousands of point-of-sale elements and racks were produced, shipped, and deployed
- 100s of projects in various stages of design and commercialization
- 100s of customers
- 70+ bottlers
- 30 yearly objectives developed by management
- Multiple daily meetings with key stakeholders with no margin to work

The role was very complicated, high-pressure, and thankless at times. Chaos was the norm. The tyranny of the urgent ruled the team. Everything was a priority. Due to job stress, I began having trouble sleeping and was always worried about what challenge was around the next corner. The work was controlling me, instead of the other way around. I was burning out, dropping the ball, and not leading my team effectively.

One day, I was sitting in a meeting when someone presented a 2x2 priority grid. I'd seen the concept before but never used it. The presenter showed how the grid helped segment initiatives and prioritize them based on levels of urgency and importance:

- High Importance/High Urgency: The work that matters most. Do these first
- High Importance/Low Urgency: Valuable work that can be added to the daily routine
- Low Importance/High Urgency: Complete these quickly or delegate
- Low Importance/Low Urgency: Low-value work that should be eliminated if possible

The light bulb went off in my head. I realized that I needed to return to a fundamental practice that I'd ignored: prioritization. Then, I blocked out some white space on my calendar to think and walk through the priorities grid. I identified areas where I could invest my time, leverage my strengths, and make a difference. Once the grid was complete, I shared it with my manager, who was delighted with it. We agreed to use the document as our focal point during our weekly one-on-ones. We'd align on the priorities and what could be removed from the to-do list.

Eventually, I began to gain control of the work and my schedule. I became more productive, less stressed, and a better leader. My team noticed the difference and asked what had changed. I shared the priorities grid with them, how I used the tool, and how it helped me focus on the essential work.

If you struggle with a complex environment, need help establishing priorities, and staying focused on the work that matters most, here are a few tips.

Initiatives vs. Priorities. People confuse these two words. There can be many initiatives, but it's up to you to prioritize them. Nothing is a priority if everything is a priority.

Spending vs. Investing Time. Time is one thing that we can't manage. However, we can manage the priorities on which we focus and the corresponding level of energy we expend. When you invest, you're actively engaging in something or someone to gain a return. What if we began investing our time in the highest-impact individuals or projects, rather than just spending our time? Ask yourself, "What will give you the greatest return on my time?" and invest there.

White Space. We all need time to think. Most folks don't purposefully schedule time on their calendar to block everything out and intentionally reflect on the work that matters most. Review your daily and weekly calendars. How do you take control of your schedule and build in white space to think without distraction? It isn't easy at first, but it is worth the time.

It's not just about the tasks we tackle but how we choose and execute them that defines our success.

FROM FIREFIGHTING TO FOCUS

If you're in a chaotic work environment, you may find that your priorities get out of whack. The Eisenhower Matrix is a valuable tool for establishing and communicating priorities.

Initially, I used the matrix to prioritize my work projects and shared the prioritization with my manager. Once we gained alignment, I'd move forward. The tool also proved to be very effective in sharing my priorities with the team. Lastly, my team members adopted the matrix and used it to communicate priorities and status updates during our one-on-one discussions.

Here are some guidelines:

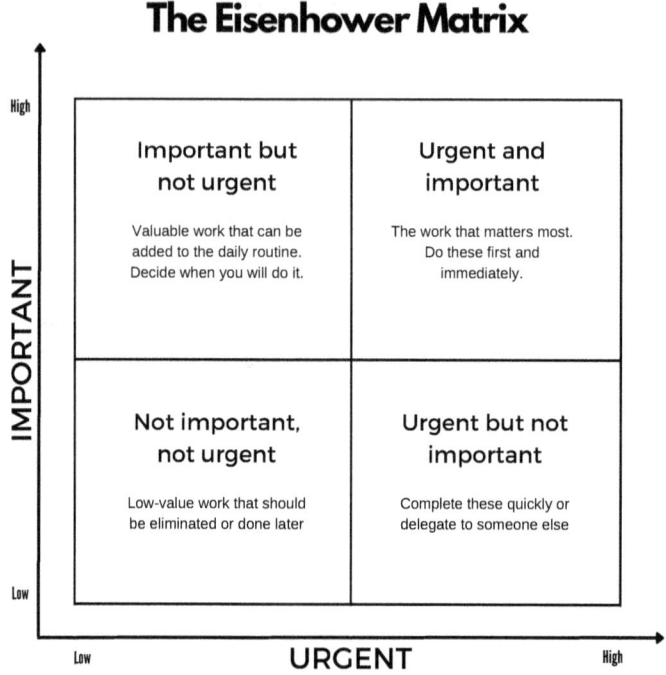

Fill in the tasks you or your team currently have to deal with

- Writing down your priorities will free your mind and allow you to focus on what's worth doing first.
- The document should be living and breathing. By that, I mean that you should capture your priorities and, once finished, remove them from the list. Update it frequently.
- Priorities may move from one quadrant to another based on circumstances.
- No one operates in a silo when working in a corporate environment or with colleagues. I found this tool helpful to align with my manager, teams, and stakeholders.

Remember, just because it's someone else's priority doesn't mean it's yours, unless it's your boss's. :-)

Reflecting on my time at The Coca-Cola Company's Strategic Merchandising Team, the lesson of prioritization stands out as a turning point. The How>What philosophy emphasizes that the way we approach our responsibilities and manage our tasks is crucial to our success. The chaos and stress I experienced were often a result of juggling too many priorities. Implementing the Eisenhower Matrix was a game-changer, allowing us to focus on what truly mattered and regain control.

SIMPLICITY IN COMMAND

Have you ever been caught in a storm of "urgent" tasks, each screaming louder than the last for your attention?

My experience at The Hershey Company, working with Milt Matthews — a retired Marine captain, Sales VP, and inductee into the Candy Hall of Fame — taught me that what truly powers priorities is their quality, not the quantity. At Hershey, three clear priorities ruled the roost: Make your plan, control your costs, and develop your people. This wasn't just a to-do list but a guide to winning the "war" and not just the battles.

Leadership is not about spreading yourself thin; it's about planting the right seeds in the right soil. It's about understanding that a priority, by definition, can't be one of a crowd. It stands alone and commands focus. And if you switch up these "priorities" too often, it only leads to confusion and frustration.

What if you could take your sprawling list of priorities and whittle it down to the essence? What are the two or three keystones that will hold up the bridge to your success?

OPPORTUNITY KNOCKS: DON'T SLAM THE DOOR

Imagine it's 1857, and you've set sail for a new land, seeking opportunity for you and your family. The poor economic conditions in Germany forced you to uproot and seek cheap farmland and financial freedom. The trans-Atlantic journey from Europe to America typically takes a couple of weeks, depending on the weather conditions. You face overcrowding, disease, fires, and shipwreck—all risks you are willing to take to start a new life. You are a carpenter by trade, possess a unique ability to persuade others, and have an entrepreneurial spirit.

During the voyage, you meet a man with big dreams. He's a great salesperson, and his charisma and vision woo you. He's emigrating to America to start a new business in Missouri. For some reason, he likes you and knows of your hard-working reputation. He shares his plans with you and asks you to become his business partner. You think about the invitation, but consider it too risky. You politely turn him down. Eventually, you arrive in America, purchase some farmland, and start your mildly successful business, wondering what might have been. This decision is driven more by fear than by insight. Instead of carefully evaluating the opportunity, internal hesitation clouded the ability to prioritize long-term potential over short-term stability.

A missed opportunity? Maybe. But before I tell you the rest of the story, let's examine some reasons we miss opportunities, explore how to discern whether to pursue them, and what it takes to capitalize on them.

The truth is, not every opportunity is meant to be seized, but it's how we approach evaluating those opportunities that sets savvy leaders apart. Smart decision-making involves distinguishing between potential distractions and genuine priorities, a skill that demands clear thinking and sound judgment.

Questions to Ask When Evaluating Opportunities
It takes imagination, critical thinking, and faith to capture or decline an opportunity. Adjusting your frame of mind when opportunities arise will enable you to evaluate objectively. Here are some questions to consider.

1. What are the potential outcomes, positive or negative? Think about the possible results a year from now, five years from now, and the consequences. What's the best that can happen, and what's the worst-case scenario? Are you willing to accept the outcomes?
2. What are the opportunity costs? Explore the potential loss or gain if an opportunity is not captured versus other alternatives. If you follow one opportunity, what other opportunities are you excluding, and at what potential cost?
3. Does the opportunity fit with your core values? If the opportunity causes you to compromise your values, ethics, or morals, say no. You want to be in a position where your values and opportunities are aligned.
4. Does it fit with your long-range goals? Determine if the opportunity aligns with what you ultimately want to accomplish.
5. Does the opportunity coincide with your strengths? Operating within your strengths will provide a more likely path to success; operating out of weaknesses won't.
6. Will you regret capitalizing on the opportunity or turning it down? Regret is a negative feeling that arises when thinking about a decision and, if made differently, would have produced a different outcome. A no-regret decision means making a choice and not looking back. A regretful decision is one that you make, and you remain uncertain about the outcome.

7. What does your inner circle say about the opportunity? Lay out the facts, pros and cons, and don't lead your advisors to a conclusion. You're looking for unbiased confirmation and perhaps even better ideas.
8. What does your gut tell you? Intuition is a powerful thing. If there is a "check" in your soul, check it out.
9. For the person of faith, what is God's direction? He speaks to his followers through the Bible, prayer, through others, and sometimes through circumstances. What are you doing to seek his input?

The Rest of the Story
According to my family lore, my great-great-great-grandfather, August Wilhelm Kotzepher (whom we'll refer to as Kotzy for short), emigrated from Germany to America in 1857. He had dreams of buying land, starting a business, and settling down in St. Louis, Missouri. He encountered Adolphus Busch during the trans-Atlantic voyage. After getting to know each other, Mr. Busch offered Kotzy the opportunity to become a partner in a beer business he was starting. I'm not sure what was brewing in Kotzy's mind at the time, but he declined. Kotzy wanted to start a furniture business, and the prospect of getting into the beer business wasn't that appealing. Adolphus Busch went on to co-found the beer giant, Anheuser-Busch. Sadly, no one's ever heard of Kotzepher furniture.

Looking from the outside in, Kotzy missed the opportunity of a lifetime, and our family always laughs about it—at least my generation.

But how about you? What will you do when opportunity strikes? Will you be able to quiet the negative internal influences? Will you know how to evaluate the opportunity?

The How>What philosophy teaches us that the way we approach potential opportunities is as crucial as the opportunities themselves. By overcoming internal barriers like fear, risk aversion, anxiety, and doubt, and by thoughtfully evaluating each prospect through critical questions and seeking wise counsel, we position ourselves for success.

MASTERING DECISION-MAKING AND PRIORITIZATION

I've witnessed this transformation occur countless times in my speaking engagements and training sessions—leaders transitioning from chaos to clarity by mastering decision-making and prioritization. If you're the leader who lets deadlines whoosh by, you're missing out on a chance to rise above the noise. Remember, it's the quality of our actions and the thoughtfulness behind them that truly make a difference.

PRINCIPLE
It's not about doing more;
it's about doing the *right* more

QUESTIONS

What are the top three tasks or decisions that currently occupy your time? Are they truly the most important, or have you fallen into the trap of focusing on what's urgent over what's impactful?

_____
_____
_____

Think about a recent decision you made under pressure. Did you approach it thoughtfully, or did you react to the chaos around you? How might a more strategic approach have changed the outcome?

_____
_____
_____

If you could focus on just one high-impact priority this week, what would it be? How will you ensure that it gets the attention it deserves?

_____
_____
_____

CHAPTER 10

Plans Don't Win

"Plans are only good intentions unless they immediately degenerate into hard work"

– PETER DRUCKER

True leaders are an endangered species.

Despite 70% of executives agreeing that strategic thinking is a critical skill for their success, less than a third of leaders have ever received formal training on how to develop it.[48] The gap isn't just an oversight—it's a significant vulnerability in the future leadership pipeline. Without the ability to think strategically, today's managers are unprepared to lead through the complexities of tomorrow's challenges.

Leadership is so much more than just having a brilliant idea; it's about *how* you—and your team—turn that idea into reality.

MIND OVER MATTER, ALWAYS

Albert Einstein, a man who knew a thing or two about thinking (you know, splitting atoms, redefining physics, easy stuff), once said, "Thinking is hard work; that's why so few do it." I'll go one step further. Not only do most people avoid thinking, but many don't know *how* to do it effectively. And that's where we get into trouble—when we're stuck trying to solve life's complex problems using grammar school math.

Speaking of math, my dad, a Ph.D. in Applied Mathematics from Caltech and the sharpest mind I've known, would often say, "Schools teach you what to think, not how to think." Need proof? Consider some of the misconceptions people believed:

- *The Earth is Flat.* For centuries, people believed this until actual "thought leaders" in Greece and Rome disproved the misconception through celestial observation. In hindsight, it's easy to see how the masses ignored the universe around them and swallowed the flat-earth myth without critical thinking.
- *Spontaneous Generation.* Out of a chapter from *Ripley's Believe It or Not*, people used to believe that organisms could spontaneously arise from living matter, like flies emerging from rotting meat. Louis Pasteur's experiments debunked the falsehood, proving that only life generates life. He never explained why God made flies in the first place, but I digress.
- *Phrenology.* It was once believed that a person's personality traits could be determined by the shape or bumps on their head. Science later discredited the misconception, finding that brain function, rather than skull shape, influences cognitive abilities and behavior.

My dad is right. Most people just assume that what is taught or repeated is the truth. If you can't form an opinion, anticipate outcomes, or break down complex issues, it's like trying to solve a Rubik's Cube with your eyes closed—frustrating, time-consuming, and more than a little awkward.

The good news? Thinking can be learned. Yes, we're all capable of sharpening those mental tools. God made us in his image, and we are wired for it. He's given you the capacity to reason, evaluate, and separate fact from fiction. To grow as a leader, here are eight mental tools you can use to help you tackle whatever challenge you face this week.

- *Analytical:* You know that friend who takes ten minutes to order coffee, breaking down each ingredient like it's a scientific experiment? That's analytical thinking—using comprehensive data, you can break down the complex into simple, detectable patterns, and develop insights.
- *Critical:* Here's where you stop taking everything at face value (sorry, social media). You carefully evaluate information, determine what's relevant, and interpret data when making decisions. You can separate the noise from the signal and focus on what matters. It's like putting on a pair of glasses that let you see through the hype.
- *Creative:* You can imagine problems or issues in a new way and generate ideas. Instead of following the usual approach, creative thinking lets you zig when others zag. You can also offer a fresh perspective with unconventional solutions through brainstorming.
- *Strategic:* This is the kind of thinking that prompts you to consider not just the next move, but also the one after that. It's chess, not checkers. You can synthesize information, assess opportunities and threats, and imagine a future direction.
- *Systems:* You know how pulling one thread can unravel an entire sweater? Systems thinking is the ability to understand how different parts of a system interact and influence one another—whether it's a business model, a team, or a project. If like me, have you ever tried to assemble IKEA furniture without reading the instructions? You get this one.
- *Lateral*: This is about approaching problems from new and unconventional angles. Instead of following the conventional path, lateral thinkers explore uncharted territory and

find solutions that others might overlook. It's like discovering a shortcut that no one has seen.
- *Reflective*: Look at this as your built-in rearview mirror. Reflective thinking involves taking the time to evaluate past actions, decisions, and experiences, learning from them, and harnessing the hindsight for today's challenge.
- *Ethical*: This one is simple, yet profound, and tempting to skip. It's the moral compass that helps you decide not only what you *can* do but what you *should* do. Spoiler alert: it's not just about profits—it's about purpose.
- *Conceptual*: Sometimes you need to zoom out. Way out. This involves thinking beyond the immediate and concrete, understanding how specific ideas and concepts fit into a larger framework. Conceptual thinking lets you see the forest, not just the trees.

Next time you have a decision to make or a problem to solve, don't rely on muscle memory. Try some new approaches and bring your team in on the fun!

It's not just *what* you think, it's *how* you think that makes the difference. Strategy doesn't appear out of thin air; it's born from deliberate, informed thought.

FROM BOARD GAMES TO COLA WARS

I loved playing the board game Risk when I was a kid. It may sound geeky, but my friends and I would spend hours trying to conquer the world. Players deploy and maneuver their armies, attack opponents, and fortify their positions to gain an advantage. The battle continues until one player has eliminated all opponents and controls every territory on the board. The game teaches long-range planning, resource management, risk assessment, adaptability, diplomacy, alliances, and territorial control. (And I learned where Kamchatka is.)

The game of Risk sums up the cola wars between Coke and Pepsi. Each company battles for market share, revenues, and profits. It's a war that I fought for over twenty years, even in restaurants.

"Sorry we don't have Coke. Is Pepsi okay?"

"No! It's not. C'mon kids, we're leaving."

Well, I never did that, but when dining with work associates or family, we'd always choose a restaurant based on whether they served Coke or not. You don't bite the hand that feeds you. Or better yet, you don't spit in the drink that's quenching your thirst. Of course, Carla, my wife, has a tad of a rebellious streak in her. She'd sneak Diet Mountain Dews any time she could. Come to think of it, Carla even bought a Snickers (they're literally from Mars) at the Harrisburg airport vending machine when we relocated for my role at Hershey Chocolate HQ. Stickin' it to the man, as the saying goes. Back to the battle.

Most people aren't familiar with what's called "The Coca-Cola System." The System is comprised of many contributors, including bottling partners and customers. The bottling partners own franchise territories in which they have the right to produce, sell, and distribute Coca-Cola products. In its simplest form, The Coca-Cola Company (TCCC) produces concentrate and sells it to its bottling partners. The bottling partners add ingredients and package the resulting beverages in many forms, including bottles and cans. The bottling partner then sells and distributes the product to multiple outlets (e.g., supermarkets, convenience stores, restaurants, etc.). In other words, TCCC produces Coca-Cola concentrate and sells it to a bottling partner. The bottling partner adds water, CO_2, and other ingredients to create the Coca-Cola beverage, puts it in a bottle or can, ships it to a store, and places it on the shelf.

That's where supply and demand meet. A shopper will purchase a Coke for a variety of reasons, and ultimately, the Coke is enjoyed by a consumer. The demand might be for a specific package, whether it's ice cold, a social media ad, or a particular meal occasion. It's TCCC's role in collaboration with its bottling partners to create consumer demand. That's the fun part about working with Coke. We sell emotional thirst refreshment.

TCCC and its bottling partners are mutually dependent. The company creates consumer demand, while bottling partners fulfill the supply. I stood right smack dab in the middle for many years as a representative, working with our bottling partners to develop local market plans that delivered revenue, profit, and market share growth. Hence, the Cola wars.

Both Coke and Pepsi employees woke up every morning wanting to win.

WONDERS AND BLUNDERS OF MARKET MASTERY

Once plans were approved by bottling partner leadership, I'd travel from market to market, presenting the plans to local salespeople and merchandisers, informing and inspiring them to achieve executional excellence. It was never a question of whether or not we would sell Coke and its vast array of products. It was a question of how much. And how much depended on how we performed. So, let's play a few rounds of Wonders and Blunders and see if you can guess which was the outcome, and why. And I'll add my twelve strategic planning steps along the way.

- *Coca-Cola C2.* There was a crazy, no-carb craze circa 2003-2004. A wide range of consumer products were launched without carbs. A funny thing was that manufacturers charged more for the no-carb products, and even more amusing was that consumers were willing to pay for them. I get it. After I kissed Hershey goodbye, I was twenty pounds overweight. So, during my first year at Coke, I decided to try the Atkins diet – no carbs – for thirty days. I only ate protein – bacon and eggs for breakfast, turkey roll-ups for lunch, and steak for dinner. No Cokes, no chips, no crackers, and certainly no candy. The pounds melted away, and I felt great. By the way, I've kept the weight off for twenty-five years. Coca-Cola decided to get into the game by introducing a reduced-calorie version of Coke, thinking there was consumer demand. The brand team created a smaller package but charged a higher price for it. I remember getting the Coke C2 plans right before Easter and spending the holiday developing plans that were due the following Monday. I wasn't happy about it, but I'd hit my planning stride with a string of successful product and packaging launches. The C2 launch would be the best one yet. TCCC and our bottling partners also went all in. We created tremendous marketing and execution plans. Actually, I think it's one of the best new product launches I've ever been a part of. We replaced all the Coca-Cola displays with Coca-Cola C2—a smaller product with a different taste, at a higher price… what could possibly go wrong? The consumer demand never materialized. *Why buy a C2 when you can buy Diet Coke?* Eventually, Coke C2 faded into the land of forgotten brands. How we flawlessly executed the launch couldn't save a product built on a flawed strategy, proving that even the best execution can't overcome a fundamental disconnect with consumer demand.

Strategic planning step 1: *Be curious.* One of our growth behaviors was Curiosity because it spurred innovation and thinking. Ask all the usual questions. Be an investigative reporter. Who, what, when, where, why, and how. Go further with questions like "What if?" and "Why not?" But in this case, we missed the boat because we weren't curious enough about what our customers thought. Some simple, low-cost focus groups could have prevented a blunder.

- *Coke Zero.* Hands down, the best brand launch I was involved in. Coke Zero delivered on taste. Diet Coke didn't. But that was on purpose. When Diet Coke was launched in 1982, its concentrate (a different formula) and taste were intended to be distinct from those of Coca-Cola. And boy was it. I consider Diet Coke an acquired taste. The company was concerned that if Diet Coke tasted too much like Coke, the new brand would cannibalize the flagship brand. And sweetener technology was still in its early stages, not enabling a Coca-Cola taste when replacing sugar. (That's probably more than you want to know.) But fast-forward to 2005, and a genius in the brand department asked, 'What if?' and Coke Zero was born. It has the same concentrate as Coca-Cola and uses an artificial sweetener blend. It has taste *and* no calories. A winner! I've always said that if something tastes good, people will buy it—but it's how we positioned Coke Zero to fit consumer needs that truly made it a success.

Strategic Planning Step 2: *Define the Problem.* Clearly identify the challenge you need to solve. Understanding the problem is the first step in developing an effective strategy. Ask yourself: What is the issue at hand? Why is it important? What are the underlying causes? Then, create a problem statement starting with "How might we?" Coke Zero was, and is, a wonder, because we offered a targeted solution to a market desire.

- *Fridge Pack.* Coke 12-ounce cans were once sold in a 3x4 carton configuration and didn't easily fit in a refrigerator nor dispense easily. In 2002, a different 2x6 configuration was introduced. Why? Because when Cokes are cold, they are more likely to be consumed. If you stick a fridge pack in the fridge, it's like having a vending machine in your refrigerator. Brilliant! We tested the package in my Alabama territory, and I was responsible for developing the marketing plan. Things didn't go smoothly at first, but we worked out the kinks and the package was launched nationwide. The tricky part was that Coke didn't own the idea of the package shape, and after the fridge pack's success, Pepsi and other manufacturers jumped on board. The Fridge Pack innovation revolutionized the way consumers store and enjoy soda, proving that how you solve simple consumer problems can lead to enduring success.

    Strategic Planning Step 3: *Define Objectives.* Clearly articulate your strategic objectives. What are you aiming to achieve? Ensure your goals are specific, measurable, achievable, relevant, and time-bound (SMART). Defining clear objectives provides direction and a framework for decision-making. Fridge packs were a wonder, simply because they hit the objective—in the market and in the refrigerator.

- *Vault.* This brand was a lot of fun, but the investment level required to compete with Mountain Dew from PepsiCo was unsustainable. Vault tasted better, had a lower price point, and had more caffeine than Mountain Dew. All the features we thought consumers wanted. But those darn Mountain Dew drinkers, my wife included, are stubborn (okay, *loyal*). Vault made an initial impact, but TCCC and its bottling partners discontinued the brand due to the enormous investment required to support it. History repeats itself, or at least rhymes. The same thing happened to Surge and Citra. The fun part was that Knoxville was a high citrus market, meaning consumers love their Mountain Dew and Sun Drop. I participated in developing the marketing and execution plans. Why fun? The brand team poured all kinds of money into the market, and we got to do a lot of cool stuff to drive the brand. A consumer packaging dream. And speaking of PepsiCo, I'll just get this off my chest. Wouldn't it be great to start a company that simply copies everything the market leader did? Am I bitter, or is it my expired cache of Vault talking? I digress. How we failed with Vault taught us to find new ways to compete using the Coca-Cola brand, proving that when a direct challenge falters, there are alternative strategies to win with familiar strengths.

Strategic Planning Step 4: *Scan the Horizon.* Analyze market trends, consumer behavior, and the competitive landscape to identify potential threats and opportunities. Keeping an eye on the big picture helps you stay ahead of the curve. Vault was a blunder because we didn't correctly assess the strength of our competitor. Sure, I love David and Goliath stories, but throwing a rock at a giant is not a one-size-fits-all strategy.

- *McCafé*. The Coca-Cola North America President at the time committed to bottling McDonald's McCafé as a shelf-stable, ready-to-drink coffee. The brand was nowhere near the category leader, Starbucks. We already offered Dunkin' Donuts RTD coffee, and it sold reasonably well. However, McCafé struggled, and it didn't look good to

McDonald's. Our on-shelf penetration and display coverage were abysmal. Eventually, McCafé achieved the distribution and display targets promised to McDonald's, making the CCNA President look good. But the product was bad to the last drop and was discontinued. How we executed McCafé couldn't overcome a weak brand proposition in a market dominated by Starbucks, showing that no matter how well you manage relationships, it is how you connect with consumers that ultimately drives success.

Strategic Planning Step 5: *Generate Insights.* Go beyond just analyzing data. Look for patterns and connections that generate useful insights. Synthesizing this information can lead to valuable learning and strategic opportunities. This blunder could have been avoided if we had paid more attention to consumer opinions than to those of the C-suite. Sorry. Not sorry.

- *16-oz Plastic Bottle.* My bottling partner didn't think it would work. During the Great Recession, Coke sales slumped, and TCCC introduced a smaller bottle than the market-dominant 20-oz plastic bottle. The 20-ounce package was the most profitable in our bottling partners' portfolio. They didn't want to introduce a package that would cannibalize its sales. That's where facts and influence played a role. We developed a strategy where the 16-oz bottle was only placed in coolers or barrels in the front of a Convenience store outlet – in an area we called the golden triangle, which included the barrel, the front door, and the cash register. *If it's cold, it's sold.* The 16-oz was within an arm's reach of desire, and the smaller bottle was just $0.99. My bottling partner agreed to test the new bottle for 90 days, and guess what? The plan worked. The analysis showed that the 16-oz bottle generated incremental sales and dollars. How we met consumers where they were during the Great Recession, with an affordable 16-oz bottle placed strategically in high-traffic areas, turned economic challenges into a sales opportunity.

Strategic Planning Step 6: *Define the 'From-To' and implications.* Clearly articulate your current state and desired future state. Understand the impact of transitioning from current results to anticipated outcomes, including the time, people, and financial resources required. These bottles were a wonder because we saw a clear benefit in the from-to equation.

- *Tab Energy/KMX.* Two energy drinks, same sad story. I recall when Tab Energy drink for women was launched; the brand manager rode through the national sales meeting on a motorcycle, wearing a pink boa. Yes, really. Before that, KMX was introduced as Coke's first energy drink. Trivia time: When first introduced, Coke was the original energy drink. All that caffeine and sugar certainly provides a lift. To put it briefly, KMX lived a short life, which included some legal hot water with a radio station of the same name, and never gained traction against competitors like Monster and Red Bull. The only people who drank KMX were TCCC employees after a long night in Key West. As for Tab Energy, let's just say the company was left with a hefty tab. The energy drink was ahead of its time, trying to compete in a male-driven category. Tab Energy and KMX couldn't compete with powerhouse brands, proving that how you position yourself in a competitive landscape determines whether you'll stand out or fade away. And in a classic case of "if you can't beat them, join them," The Coca-Cola System solidified its position in the energy category by entering into a distribution agreement with Monster, turning competition into a partnership that allowed them to compete more effectively.

Strategic Planning Step 7: *Focus resources.* Strategic thinking is about making decisions. Saying yes to one thing often means saying no to another. Align your resources to your strategic intent and be ready to adjust as necessary. These products were blunders because, in hindsight, you can't beat a monster or red bull by waving a few red flags. It takes a ton of focus and resources for a long-term commitment.

- *Share a Coke*. The promotion was launched by Coca-Cola in Australia in 2011 and became an iconic campaign globally. The premise was simple yet innovative: replace the iconic Coca-Cola logo on bottles and cans with 150 of the most popular names in Australia. This personalization made the product feel unique and personal to consumers, encouraging them to find and share bottles with their own names or those of friends and family. In 2014, we introduced Share a Coke in the US, and the promotion drove incredible revenue, profit, and market share growth. We couldn't believe shoppers would literally rummage around in a bin looking for their name. But they did. Our Strategic Merchandising Team, which I've mentioned a few times, even received the prestigious Display of the Year award for the Share a Coke Contour bottle display, the highest recognition in the Marketing at Retail Industry (POPAI). Personalization drove sales of our most profitable 20-oz bottle, proving that how you engage consumers can turn a simple idea into a major success.

Strategic Planning Step 8: *Create Strategic Pillars.* Identify the key areas that will support your overall strategy. Strategic pillars are the foundational elements that guide your efforts and resource allocation. They should align with your objectives and reflect your core priorities. Just think about all the potential disasters that might arise from putting hundreds of names on cans. This initiative was a true wonder, and it's a wonder that the thousands of logistical considerations came together seamlessly. The amount of planning was staggering.

- *Vanilla Coke.* The first Coca-Cola flavor variant was introduced in 2002. We launched Vanilla Coke soon after I started, and it was one of the first brand launches for which I developed local plans and inspired execution. I remember standing on a busy intersection in Montgomery, Alabama, handing out samples to drivers on the launch day. Vanilla Coke had a rocky journey. It sold well initially but soon tapered off. The brand was discontinued, but TCCC revived it in 2007 in response to consumer demand.[49] I led the local market activation planning and used Justin Timberlake's "Sexy Back" as our theme song. "We're bringing Vanilla back..." We applied consistent pressure and stuck with Vanilla Coke, ensuring it remained popular, demonstrating how persistence with a brand can determine its market sustainability.

Strategic Planning Step 9: *Draft Initiatives to Support Strategic Pillars.* Develop specific initiatives that will drive progress within each strategic pillar. These initiatives should be actionable and detailed, outlining the steps necessary to achieve the desired outcomes. Ensure they are aligned with your strategic objectives and resources. This flavor didn't just magically appear and reappear on the shelves. It took massive, detailed, and on-target marketing support. Without these initiatives, Vanilla Coke would have had the sad distinction of failing twice.

- *Diet Coke with Lemon.* I have mixed emotions about this one. It tasted more like Diet Coke with Pledge, the lemon-scented dust spray (not that I ever tasted it). This was TCCC's first flavored cola line extension and failed miserably. But our Alabama team did a great job on the launch and showed that we could execute with excellence, resulting in our being awarded the Fridge Pack test. How we delivered Diet Coke with Lemon missed the mark on taste, demonstrating that no matter how well you execute, if the product itself doesn't resonate with consumers, success is impossible. I repeat, "if it tastes good, people will buy it." – Diet Coke with Lemon, not so much.

  Strategic Planning Step 10: *Collaborate with others.* Embrace diverse perspectives. If you're the smartest person in the room, you're in the wrong room. Strategic thinkers seek input from others to strengthen and refine their strategies. Bottom line: Lemon was a lemon and a blunder simply because we didn't have the guts to openly discuss the product.

- *Vitaminwater / Smartwater.* Purchased from Glaceau in 2007. The brands infused personality into Coke's portfolio, enabling it to compete with Gatorade. By the way, one of the biggest mistakes, in my opinion, is when Warren Buffett, a TCCC board of directors member, put the kibosh on Coke purchasing Gatorade. Something about long-term returns. Pardon my language, but *Fiddlesticks!* It set Coke back years from competing in the non-carbonated arena.

"He's been a very huge influence on Coke's board," said Walter Todd, a money manager with Greenwood Capital Inc. in Greenwood, S.C., which owns 275,000 shares of Coca-Cola. "Coke might have gotten Gatorade if Buffett wasn't on the board. It was definitely a mistake — maybe the biggest one in Coke's history." In 2000, Buffett urged Coca-Cola's board to reject Daft's proposal to spend $14 billion to acquire Gatorade's parent company, Quaker Oats Co. Rival PepsiCo later bought Gatorade, and sales of the sports drink have risen at double-digit rates each year. Gatorade is the top-selling sports drink worldwide, with 80% of the market.[50]

It just goes to show that sometimes, playing it too safe can set you back. Missing out on Gatorade could have set us back, but how we rebounded with the strategic acquisition of Glaceau showed that recovery is about how you adapt and move forward.

Strategic Planning Step 11: *Execute*. A strategy only comes to life through implementation. It requires the disciplined execution of resources to achieve goals, implement initiatives, execute tactics, and make necessary adjustments. And inspect what you expect. You can't know what's going on in the market by sitting at your desk. Coke blundered because we didn't seize the moment.

What do the wonders and blunders have in common? They all required strategic planning and execution. I loved working with the brands. Some were fantastic, others were complete failures. Always a challenge in a hyper-competitive environment. I consider The Coca-Cola Company the pinnacle of consumer products. Think about it. Our brands are ubiquitous and available everywhere. But seriously, you can travel to France's Mont Saint-Michel and buy a Coke Zero in a little café. You can enjoy a Coke in Istanbul's Grand Bazaar. And you can sip on a Coke in Lima, Peru. Which leads me to my final step, which has been key to success.

> **Strategic Planning Step 12:** *Measure Progress.* Develop a scorecard that includes key metrics. Then, review often and course-correct when necessary.

THE FRENEMY IN THE COOLER

I can't call this book complete without taking a stand on a divisive subject. Here's a word on Dr. Pepper. No, I do not, and have never wanted to be, a "Pepper." I don't get it. And from a business perspective, the brand was a constant thorn in my side. Our "how" couldn't have been more different. The problem wasn't just that they were a competitor (owned by Keurig Green Mountain, not Coke or Pepsi as many would assume); it was the internal competition they created within our own system. A lot of our bottling partners distributed both Coke and Dr. Pepper, which meant the pesky Dr. was constantly jockeying for bottlers' attention and resources that should've been focused on growing our brands.

We were focused on building long-term partnerships with bottlers, collaborating on business plans, traveling with leadership, and driving long-term growth. Dr. Pepper? They threw around enticing incentives and popped in only when they needed something.

They didn't offer thought leadership or proactive collaboration. Dr. Pepper was like that girlfriend or boyfriend who showed up when it suited them. And my bottling partners? They said "better friend than foe" – better to have them on the team or in the cooler than not. Ugh.

WHAT IF PLANS GO DOWN THE TOILET?
While in Rome, I stayed at a hotel where the toilet paper cover read, "Backup plan." It was funny at the time, but back at Coca-Cola, running without a backup plan wasn't amusing—it was chaotic. We never had a solid Plan B. It was like realizing you're at the end of the roll with no spare in sight—an uncomfortable, reactive scramble.

When things didn't go as planned, we'd either override the strategy or rewrite it altogether, trying to close the gaps. Corporate would release funds; we'd have to convince the bottlers to buy into the new plan, and then we'd execute it under pressure. Sure, these needs often spurred innovation, but the constant fire drills put a lot of strain on the System. It didn't have to be that way.

If I could go back, I'd have made sure we anticipated challenges and had backup plans ready to go before we launched—just like checking for an extra roll beforehand. That's what strategic thinking is really about—being prepared for every scenario. The How>What philosophy? It's not just about having a great plan on paper; it's about how you plan for the unexpected.

IDEAS ARE CHEAP; EXECUTION ISN'T
A brilliant strategy without execution is like a blueprint without a builder—so much untapped potential. From my experience with brands like Coke Zero, Vitaminwater, and the Share a Coke campaign, it wasn't the brilliance of the strategy alone that created

value. It was how we executed in the market that made all the difference. Without flawless execution, even the best ideas remain just that—ideas.

Clarity in Communication Prevents Chaos. During the Fridge Pack rollout, our clear communication with local bottlers and retailers helped everyone understand their roles and expectations. Yes, there were hiccups, but once we addressed the issues and improved communication, the new package drove sales and profits. No matter how well we plan, constant communication and iteration are essential for quality execution.

You Can't Win if You Don't Measure Success. The Share a Coke campaign was a bubbling success, not only because of the personalization but also because we established clear goals and measured performance at every stage. Sales metrics and consumer engagement broke records. We didn't just launch and move to the next project; we tracked every detail. Measuring progress and course correcting are crucial to ensure quality and create value.

Adaptability Turns Obstacles into Opportunities. We had to alleviate the bottler's doubts about the new 16-oz plastic bottle. So, we adjusted our marketing strategy based on real-time data. By adapting, the 16-oz bottle became a game-changer.

Sweat The Small Stuff. Execution isn't about the big, flashy moves—it's about mastering the details. I learned that firsthand with the launch of Vanilla Coke. Even for a small local event, every detail counted. From the handouts to the choice of music, the little things made the experience memorable. It's those intentional extras that turn good ideas into real success.

Execution isn't just the final step in a process—it's the culmination of every thought, decision, and problem solved along the way.

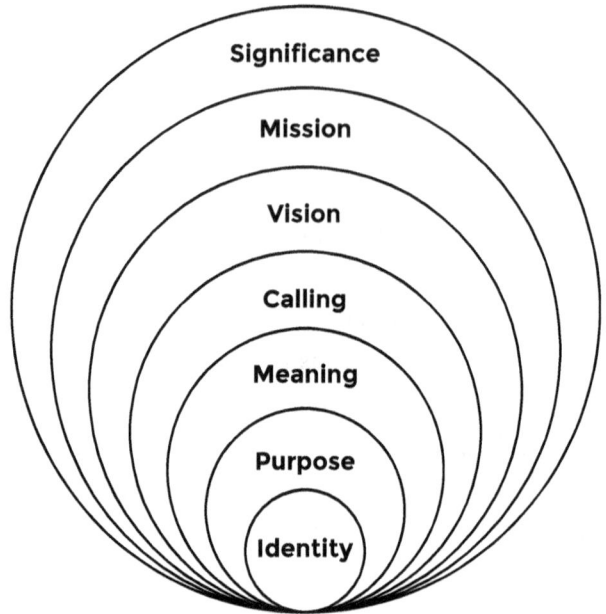

BRIDGING STRATEGY AND EXECUTION TO SIGNIFICANCE

Strategy and execution aren't just about hitting the mark—they're the bridge that leads to significance. It's not enough to have a bold strategy (what); the real impact comes from *how* you execute that strategy with precision and purpose. This is where the How>What philosophy comes to life.

Just like the journey from Identity to Purpose, Vision, and ultimately Significance, strategy and execution make the lasting difference. Execution creates legendary results.

Execution is not a launch. Bold strategies set the stage, but relentless execution brings them to life. And the real key to lasting success? Constantly refining and improving along the way.

My twelve strategic planning steps:
1. Be curious.
2. Define the Problem.
3. Define Objectives.

4. Scan the Horizon.
5. Generate Insights.
6. Define the 'From-To' and implications.
7. Focus resources.
8. Create Strategic Pillars.
9. Draft Initiatives to Support Strategic Pillars.
10. Collaborate with others.
11. Execute.
12. Measure Progress.

These strategic approaches are pretty simple, right? But the most important part is applying them—intentionally and daily. When I was part of the capabilities team, we were responsible for training customer and bottling partner representatives on how to develop a strategic plan. We created the process and templates. Most folks saw them as paper exercises. The few who grasped it understood that we were teaching them how to think strategically, much like the game of Risk taught me when I was young: long-range planning, resource management, risk assessment, adaptability, diplomacy, alliances, and territorial control.

PRINCIPLE
Strategize boldly, execute relentlessly, improve continuously

QUESTIONS

How do you and your team create a strategy? Reflect on how your approach to problem-solving and critical thinking impacts the effectiveness of the strategy you create. Are you more focused on what needs to be done or on how you approach the thinking process itself?

_____
_____
_____

Consider a recent strategic initiative. Did you emphasize how the strategy would be implemented, or did you focus more on the end goals? How can you improve your strategic process to align with the How>What philosophy?

_____
_____
_____

Think about a recent project or service launch. Were you intentional about how you measured results and improved your plan? How can you enhance the how in your execution process?

_____
_____
_____

CHAPTER 11

Change or Be Changed

"No one likes to change,
except a baby with a wet diaper."
—AUTHOR UNKNOWN

Have you ever considered what it takes to truly transform a living space—or a life? My wife, Carla, and I embarked on an unexpected journey that not only transformed a room in our house but also deepened our insights into life and leadership. Our adventure began when we were chosen to appear on the Reality TV show "Run My Renovation," a unique experience where viewers' votes determined everything from the design to the details of our primary bathroom makeover.

From afar, our bathroom seemed fine, but a closer look revealed its flaws: peeling cabinets, mismatched doors, a non-draining shower, and a trip-hazard doorway. The DIY Network audience took charge, selecting everything from the shower tiles and hardwood floors to an expansive bathtub and fresh paint, transforming the space into one that's stunning both up close and from a distance. It wasn't until we were in the spotlight that I really noticed just how run-down our bathroom had become. I had become so accustomed to it that I felt comfortable; as a result, the whole process turned out to be a humbling experience. I realized I needed to be open to other viewpoints and accept the discomfort that change brings.

The process, condensed into a thirty-minute episode, actually spanned several days, with a bustling crew taking over our home. We were involved in minor decisions and reactions on camera, but the heavy lifting was left to the professionals after the director's cut. The result? A primary bathroom we absolutely love, showcasing a total transformation.

This renovation got me thinking about the parallels between transforming a physical space and personal transformations in leadership and life. Just like our bathroom required a complete overhaul, there are times in life when we realize that surface-level changes aren't enough. True transformation goes deeper, whether it's in our careers, relationships, or personal growth.

This journey through renovation opened my eyes to the essence of leadership: the power of positive influence and the ripple effect it has on those around us. As leaders, our personal transformation can have a profound impact on the culture of our teams, communities, and organizations.

CHANGE STARTS WITH YOU

Tolstoy said it best: "Everyone wants to change the world, but no one wants to change themselves."[51] We need to understand who we are, what drives us, and our purpose. That's the heart of how we lead—it's about being before doing. It's grounded in your identity, purpose, meaning, vision, and mission. Without that solid foundation, leading change in others doesn't work.

Leading change isn't about having the perfect strategy or just checking boxes. It's about connecting with people and understanding their challenges. They don't need more orders; they need someone who relates to their questions and is ready to face uncertainty with them. Leading through change takes courage.

And here's the key: integrity. If people don't trust you to follow through, they won't follow you. Trust is the foundation of leadership.

The difference between change management and change leadership is simple. Change management is the "what"—the plans, the processes, the tactics. But change leadership? That's the "how."

If you're not leading the charge, you'll find yourself playing catch-up. But where do we start?

TRANSFORMED LIVES, TRANSFORMED CULTURES

Once we've embraced personal transformation, the real magic begins. That internal shift—the one that aligns us with our identity, purpose, and vision—starts to ripple outward, impacting everything around us. Function follows formation. It's not just about being transformed; it's about doing something meaningful with that transformation.

Leaders who have gone through personal change can't help but influence those around them. That internal change compels external action. We lead differently, we inspire differently, and we approach challenges with a deeper understanding of what it takes to make an impact. This is where transformational leadership really kicks in. It's leadership driven by personal growth, but aimed at creating something bigger than ourselves.

When we step into action, we become catalysts for cultural change. Our transformed lives naturally begin to transform the cultures we interact with—whether in our workplaces, our communities, or even on a larger scale. And it all starts with that internal transformation.

As Chuck Colson said in How Now Shall We Live?, "Cultures can be renewed—even those typically considered the most corrupt and intractable. But if we are to restore our world, we first have to shake off the idea that our personal decisions don't ripple outward. Every choice contributes to the moral and cultural climate in which we live." [52]

This is the essence of transformational leadership. Leaders who have transformed themselves don't just manage people; they inspire them. They don't just respond to change; they drive it forward with a vision for something greater. The cultures they lead reflect the change they've undergone themselves.

So, how do we start to transform cultures? By transforming ourselves first, and then allowing that transformation to shape how we lead. Whether in a company or a community initiative, the real power to influence others starts from within.

Leading change isn't just about implementing new systems, organizations, or strategies. It's about leading by example. Once you've embraced your own transformation, you're best positioned to guide others through the journey with purpose, empathy, and integrity. That's when change becomes so much more-it becomes transformational. It becomes a movement.

INSPIRING A MOVEMENT, NOT JUST MANAGING IT

Living in Atlanta, you can't help but feel the history around you. Recently, I visited the Civil Rights Museum and took part in the Woolworth's lunch counter sit-in simulation—a profoundly moving experience. Picture this: you're a protester in the 1960s, standing up against Jim Crow laws and the absurd "separate but equal" doctrine. At the time, Black patrons could purchase food but were required to stand at the snack bar, while the dining area was reserved exclusively for whites. It was this kind of injustice that fueled nonviolent resistance.

The simulation places you right in that moment. You sit at a replica lunch counter, put on earphones, and instantly you're surrounded by the sounds of clattering dishes and insults being hurled. The stool beneath you vibrates with the sensation of being kicked. The whole experience forces you to ask yourself: How long could I have lasted in the face of such hatred and intimidation? It drives home just how much people were willing to endure for their mission of change.

Jim Crow laws institutionalized this, but they did much more – they transformed every aspect of life, and, in particular, they repeatedly crushed black opportunities as a matter of course – whether in schools, restrooms, water fountains, or anything and everything else. The 1896 decision in Plessy v. Ferguson entrenched the concept of 'separate but equal,' but there was nothing equal about it. Bucking the cultural script was a dangerous and high-stakes endeavor.

Martin Luther King Jr was the face of that fight, but he was more than just a beloved icon; he was an example of transformational leadership. He wasn't managing change; he was leading it. He was creating a movement that was far more than segregation or voting rights. His goal was to shift the entire cultural mindset, and he achieved it through nonviolent resistance, demonstrating a different path forward to the world.

King created a movement that altered the course of history. His approach was much more than dynamic speeches. He mobilized people around a cause, built coalitions, led meetings and marches, and helped create a movement. He didn't attempt to control every detail but empowered others, guiding them through uncertainty and managing the inevitable resistance that comes with meaningful, lasting change.

And here's the thing: When you're leading change—whether it's in a movement, within yourself, or within your organization, you'll always face resistance. People resist change due to fear, a desire to maintain the status quo, or simply because they are uncomfortable with it. But leaders don't avoid resistance – they face it head-on.

Leading change starts with a clear vision and the courage to guide people through resistance. Leaders must strike a balance between the boldness to take the first step and the wisdom necessary to manage the process along the way.

WINNING BEYOND THE SCOREBOARD[53]

As I was writing about Martin Luther King Jr., I was reminded of a time when I heard Nick Saban refer to MLK Jr's "Street Sweeper Speech." King's message was about the dignity of labor—the idea that whatever you do, you should do it with excellence. It's a philosophy that stuck with me, especially when Saban shared how his own approach to leadership shifted over time.

Before 1998, Saban wasn't the transformational leader we recognize today. By his own admission, he was transactional—focused solely on results. If his team won, they'd get a pat on the back. If they lost, they felt the brunt of his frustration. No lessons, no growth—just outcomes. But when your leadership is purely transactional, you risk losing your team when things aren't going well, and even when you score some wins.

The turning point for Saban came during a crucial game against Ohio State. His team was 4-5 for the season, and his job at Michigan State was on the line. In that moment, he realized something had to change. Transactional leadership wasn't cutting it. If he was going to lead effectively, he needed to become a transformational leader.

Saban's focus shifted from outcomes to the process. He began focusing on long-term growth, instilling core values, and prioritizing the well-being of his team, regardless of the result. He famously taught the players to take it one play at a time, focus on what's right in front of them, and do their job. He preached resilience and growth beyond the scoreboard. That game wasn't just a win for the team but a tipping point for Saban's entire career.

He didn't just tweak a few tactics; he led a whole cultural shift. He built a case for change by shifting the focus away from winning at all costs to personal growth, unity, and purpose. Change leadership isn't just about managing a situation—it's about guiding people through transformation.

Once the team bought into the vision, they began to believe in something bigger than the next game. That's what effective change management looks like—building a framework for sustainable change and leading your people through it.

Saban's success wasn't just about what he did—it was about how he led and the mindset he cultivated. Once he shifted his focus from the results to the process (from what to how), the wins naturally followed.

CHANGE HAPPENS: ADAPT OR FAIL

I've moved twelve times, transferred colleges (CU to CSU), changed my major three times (political science, psychology, business—some say I didn't know what I wanted to be when I grew up, and I wonder at times), changed companies five times (AmSouth, Ralston Purina, Dale Carnegie, Hershey, and Coke) held 10 different jobs, not to mention countless other changes I've observed in my lifetime. My observation: There are three sure things in life: death, taxes, and change.

I've led or participated in organizational transformations, such as Coca-Cola's System of the Future initiative, which involved divesting the conglomerate bottler and re-franchising Coca-Cola Refreshments into smaller bottler territories (SOF), as well as the Merchandising Materials Transformation (MMT), where point-of-sale materials and merchandising racks were treated as products.

The SOF change was massive. "All told, during the span of 10 years, the Coca-Cola Co. and its U.S. bottling partners worked together to execute 60 (divestiture) transitions, which included 350 distribution centers, more than 50 production facilities, more than 55,000 employees and more than 1.3 billion physical cases of volume."[54]

In support of the SOF, I established and led an eight-person team. The team was accountable for geographic leadership in seventeen North American markets and delivered $4.4 billion in annual revenue.

During my tenure with the Strategic Merchandising Solutions team (where my hair turned gray and I pulled most of it out), I led a twelve-person team that managed over 20,000 elements and $120 million in expenditures across more than 20 suppliers.

Here's a harsh reality: Change management initiatives fail not because the need for change is unclear, but because of how the change is mishandled. Two-thirds of all change management initiatives fail. Why? Underestimated costs, employee resistance, and a lack of upper management communication.[55]

I learned how to manage and lead change during my time at Coke. You could say I earned a PhD in change-ology. I now conduct workshops to equip organizations for navigating their own change initiatives. And I discovered you can create positive change in your workplace, community, school, or church by following some simple steps.

Build the case. Define the change, articulate the benefits, and outline the transition from the current state to the future state. Create a clear vision and secure leadership support.

Drive Commitment. Assemble a cross-functional team (e.g., finance, manufacturing, marketing, and every step in the process) responsible for leading the change. Then, create a communication strategy that focuses on two key groups: stakeholders and those affected by the change.

- Align Key Stakeholders. Analyze their influence and interests, understand their motivations, and address concerns. Gain support by incorporating their feedback into the plan.
- Connect with the affected. Understand how the change impacts the organization and its people, using the Bridges Transition Model[56] that follows (Ending, Neutral Zone, and New Beginning) to guide them through phases from resistance to acceptance.

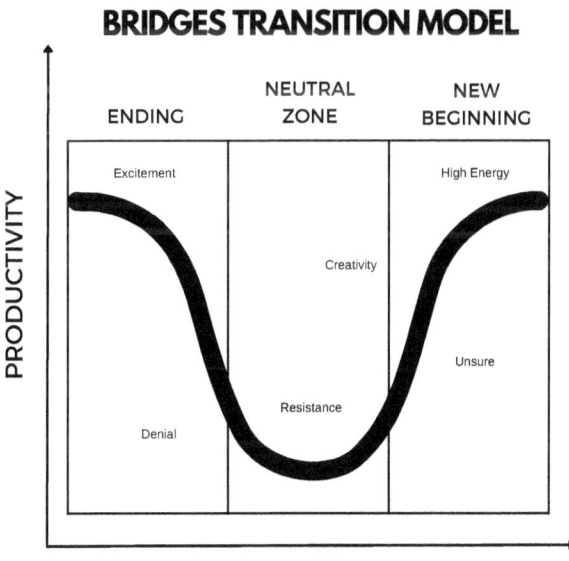

Develop the plan. Define the approach, set clear goals, and assign roles to guide the transition from the current state to the future state.

Execute and learn. Implement the plan, track progress, ask questions, and address challenges as they arise. Celebrate milestones, problem-solve issues, and capture learnings to refine the process for future leaders.

LEADING CHANGE, TITAN-STYLE

I do love movies. Who me? A shocker, I know. Which somehow brings me back to my story about Sunset Cinema and our viewing of Remember the Titans. The movie reminds me that it's more than just throwing the football in the end zone that makes for a winning football team. It's about strategy, teamwork, grit, and managing change. The 2000 movie is set circa 1971 in the city of Alexandria, Virginia, during the notorious times of desegregation (aka the racial integration of public schools). Coach Herman Boone, tasked with transforming a diverse group of players into one team, turns a football team into a community – one that's in the midst of change. Here are my Titan-style takeaways in leading change.

Build the Case

In truth, Coach Boone is not just taking over a team; he's taking over a collection of divided players. The need for change is clear, but it's not just about winning or losing football games. Boone knows the situation – a football team divided by racism – and he knows the future he wants: a football team that can act as a beacon for the entire community. The stakes could not be higher. If they don't come together, he says, it's not just about losing a game, it's about losing a chance to demonstrate the power of unity. Boone builds a compelling argument for change. He earns buy-in from his coaching staff and players by outlining the stakes

– what's at risk – and then painting a vision of a team that overcomes division and shows what could be.

Drive Commitment
The heart of change lies in commitment, both from those leading it and those experiencing it.
- Align Key Stakeholders. The relationship between Coach Boone and Coach Yoast offers a textbook example. Both, initially with different perspectives, realize that their unified front is vital for the team's success. Ensuring that influential figures are on board, understanding their motivations, and addressing their concerns can set the stage for smoother transitions.
- Connect with the Affected. The most resonant scenes in Remember the Titans are those in which teammates, once at odds, begin to understand each other. Boone's strategies, from pairing players of different races to the intense training, are about building connections. Communication must be transparent, emphasizing the reasons behind the change, addressing concerns, and spotlighting the benefits.

People will engage and commit to a change if they know: what is changing, what's not changing, why it needs to change, how they will benefit, that they will have the necessary support, tools, and training to be successful, and clear expectations.

After developing a communication strategy for those affected by the change, use the Bridge Transition Model to identify where people are in the change journey. Leaders go first. Ask yourself where you are on the transition curve. You'll need to embrace the change before you can ask your people to. Then consider where your people are on the

Transition Model and determine how to inspire them to move into the New Beginning phase.

Lastly, determine how you can encourage slow adopters to embrace the change. Studies indicate people are typically motivated to change by three motivating factors and benefits: the hope of gaining something, the fear of losing something, or the avoidance of pain. Change will only occur if the motivation to change and the perceived benefits are greater than the effort required. Here's a helpful formula.

- If Motivation (hope of gaining, fear of losing, avoiding pain) > Energy (effort required) = Change
- If Motivation (hope of gaining, fear of losing, avoiding pain) ≤ Energy (effort required) = No Change

Exercise empathy with associates who are experiencing fear or a desire to avoid pain; put yourself in their shoes, ask what's holding them back, and help them see what's in it for them. Return to why the change is needed, the vision, the plan, and the role they will play.

A few months before I retired from The Coca-Cola Company, my wife, Carla, and I attended a baseball game at the Atlanta Braves' stadium. We began discussing the future and what retirement life might look like. I could tell she was hesitant and concerned about the imminent change. Carla was in the resistant phase of the change curve and rightly so. She was concerned my mind would become mush without being involved in something meaningful. Recognizing this, I explained the Bridges' Transition Model to her. (Not sure what you talk about at sporting events, but I bet you keep your conversations a little lighter.) I asked her where she was on the curve and where she thought I was. That question was a hit. She said she was still in the neutral zone, resistant to the change. I then asked her what she needed to move to enthusiasm about my retirement. As we discussed her questions and concerns, hesitancy fell away, and her hope for this new season of life arose. Home run.

Develop the Plan
With the case for change in place and commitment gained, Coach Boone moves into action. Through tough practices, breaking down the playbook, and strategy sessions, the Titans start preparing for what's ahead. Roles are clearly defined, expectations are set, and everyone knows what's on the line. This is where the vision becomes real—each player understanding how their role fits into the bigger mission.

Execute and Learn
As we discussed in the previous chapter, execution is everything. It's where the rubber meets the road, or in the case of football, when the center meets the defensive line. Every game the Titans played testified to their preparation, unity, and adaptability. In the same way, its real-world implications become crystal clear once a change plan rolls out.

Remember the Titans isn't just a movie about football—it's a powerful lesson in change leadership. What makes the difference is the how—the strategies, connections, and leadership that drive the team forward. Whether on the field or in the boardroom, the way we approach change is what ultimately leads to success.

SURVIVING THE CORPORATE GAUNTLET

When the phone rang, I froze. And stared at it with anxious anticipation as my career flashed before my eyes. The call I'd been waiting for would reveal my future with the company. I'd been through a series of evaluations and interviews to keep my current job. As my heart began racing and sweat beads formed on my brow, I finally answered the phone.

"Hello, this is Preston."

"Hi. This is Ted. I'm calling to let you know..."

If you've ever worked in a corporate environment, you may have received a similar call. And you've experienced the effects of organizational change—uncertainty, layoffs, or downgraded compensation. I've been through fourteen restructures in my career between Hershey and Coke. I liken the process to running for Congress—every two years, you're up for re-election, and if you're elected, you begin your next campaign immediately. A musical chairs analogy also applies. We marched around the chairs until the music stopped and learned our fate.

The topsy-turvy corporate world can be exasperating and disheartening. The challenge is to remain hopeful. You might say, "But Preston, hope isn't a strategy."

Well, if hope isn't a strategy, what is it?

Hope is an expectation that a particular desire will be fulfilled, a promise will be kept, or a better future is on the horizon. Hope provides internal energy, motivation, and the courage to persevere. I've heard it said that someone can live forty days without food, four days without water, four minutes without air, and only 4 seconds without hope.[57] Why is hope such a crucial part of life and our well-being? It energizes and inspires us to keep going. Without hope, we begin to think that circumstances will only get worse, and we'll give up. How does someone remain hopeful amid constant change and challenging events?

Pray. For Christians, start by connecting with your source of hope, God. Take your concerns to him and seek his guidance.

Don't lose heart. In tough times, choose to believe that you can and will succeed. Think about your past achievements and recount your strengths. Remember, the circumstances don't define you. Jesus' words provide confidence, "In this godless world you will continue to experience difficulties. But take heart! I've conquered the world." (John 16:33b - The Message)

Manage Self-Talk. Did you know our thoughts shape our beliefs and actions? As I mentioned in chapter 7, Dancing with Wolves, our challenge is that eight out of ten thoughts are negative. Replace the lies with the truth. How? When self-doubt creeps in, and I'm experiencing despair, I've found it helpful to pause and say an affirming phrase ten times to myself. It helps change my mindset from negative to positive. For example, instead of saying to yourself, "I'm a weak person," say, "I'm a strong person." Rather than saying, "I can't do anything right," say, "I can do all things through Christ who strengthens me." The Bible says, "Summing it all up, friends, I'd say you'll do best by filling your minds and meditating on things true, noble, reputable, authentic, compelling, gracious—the best, not the worst; the beautiful, not the ugly; things to praise, not things to curse." (Philippians 4:8, The Message). If you do these things, you'll win the battle of the mind.

Keep a long-term perspective. Tough times don't last, but tough people do. The Bible says, "These hard times are small potatoes compared to the coming good times, the lavish celebration prepared for us. There's far more here than meets the eye. The things we see now are here today, gone tomorrow. But the things we can't see now will last forever" (2 Corinthians 4:17-18, The Message).

Face reality and take responsibility. Accept the fact that life can be backbreaking at times. Then, objectively evaluate your challenging circumstance and define the problem you face. What's the worst that can happen? What are all of your options? How can you improve upon the worst? Once you answer these questions, take ownership. Embrace the opportunity to change and intentionally determine to grow through the circumstance. Think, if it's to be, it's up to me. As a person of the Christian faith, I subscribe to this approach: "Work like it's up to me and trust God like it's up to him."

Plan, act, and persevere. Once you've faced reality, taken responsibility, and determined the best course of action, be intentional and go for it. Put a plan together. Develop goals and move in the direction you've chosen. Look for quick wins and build momentum. If you plan, act, and persevere, you'll begin to experience success. The road ahead will be different from what you expected, harder than you anticipated, and potentially more rewarding than you imagined. My mentor, John Maxwell says, "Everything worthwhile is uphill." Back to my phone call.

"Hello, this is Preston."

"Hi. This is Ted. I'm calling to let you know you will be retained by the company."

When I received the call, I was in the midst of my thirteenth organizational change. Once again, I struggled with all of the self-doubt and uncertainty that comes with the unsettling circumstance. But even though I didn't know what was going to happen, by this time I also had the confident expectation that no matter what the company told me, I would be just fine.

Navigating corporate change can feel like an endless rollercoaster, but maintaining hope is essential. Why am I talking about "hope and change" in a book about leadership? Because hope is a powerful force. A certain president of the United States won two elections on that platform.

MASTERING THE MESS: LEADING THROUGH CHANGE

Authentic change leadership starts from within, and your personal transformation sets the tone for everything else. How you connect with your team, handle the challenging moments, and build trust will determine whether the change you lead sticks or fades. The what—the plans and tactics—only work when grounded in a clear sense of purpose. It's simple: change, or be changed.

PRINCIPLE

Don't just manage change, lead it.

QUESTIONS

How have your experiences with change shaped your approach to leadership? What concrete steps can you take to ensure your own transformation positively influences those you lead?

_____
_____
_____

Think back to a recent change initiative you were part of. How did you tackle any resistance from your team? What strategies can you adopt in the future to create a more supportive atmosphere during transitions?

_____
_____
_____

What opportunities are before me to be an example, and step into the waters of change?

_____
_____
_____

CHAPTER 12

What's That Smell?

> "Nothing revives the past so completely
> as a smell that was once associated with it."
> – VLADIMIR NABOKOV

Ever notice how certain smells can instantly transport you to a place or moment?

I was riding my bike on a perfect day: a bright, sunny sky, 72 degrees, and a light breeze. Suddenly, I heard a rumbling behind me. A garbage truck sped past, barely missing me. In its wake, it left a stench—an inescapable mix of rotten food, spoiled diapers, and decomposing grass.

Now, contrast that with a trip my wife and I took to my favorite city, San Francisco. The sea breeze filled our senses as we drove across the Golden Gate Bridge in our convertible. As we reached Napa Valley, the sweet fragrance of grapes replaced the salty air. I took a deep breath, savoring the aroma.

CORPORATE AROMAS

I once heard a consultant say, "Culture is the smell around here."

That got me thinking: Is your organizational culture toxic, like the wake of a garbage truck? Or is it fragrant, like a vineyard in Napa Valley? More importantly, *how* did it get that way?

It's not just *what* you do that creates a culture—it's *how* you go about it. You could have all the right processes and strategies, but if the *how* is filled with toxic behaviors—such as bad communication and a lack of trust—it's like the garbage truck, leaving a stench everywhere it goes. And adding an "air freshener" to the mix never helps.

On the other hand, when leaders focus on building a foundation of trust, respect, and engagement, they create a culture that leaves a lasting impression and pleasant memories.

Just as those garbage-truck workers might become desensitized to the stench, we can become oblivious to our environment. We start accepting rotten behaviors as normal.

What does your workplace culture smell like? And *how* are you contributing to that scent?

HOW TO MANAGE BEING MICROMANAGED

My team and I were invited to a strategic business partner's corporate headquarters to brainstorm about how to innovate. I viewed the trip as an excellent opportunity to retreat, bond as a team, and shape our future.

I approached my manager, Kevin, about the opportunity. He hesitated and then said, "Most trips like these are boondoggles. Do you think you're going to accomplish anything?"

"Thanks for the vote of confidence, jerk-face," I shot back. "After all, you are the resident expert on boondoggles." Okay, that's what I *thought*.

What I actually said was, "Yes, I do. I'm confident that we'll come back with fresh ideas and take our business to the next level."

Kevin replied, "I'll tell you what, put together a plan with specific objectives, and I'll take a look. If I agree with your proposal, I'll approve the trip."

Of course, I had a plan in mind, but in all my years, I'd never been asked to submit a detailed trip plan. It seemed like a futile exercise, but I acquiesced, nonetheless.

Over the next few days, I collaborated with my team and business partner to refine our plan and get even more specific about the desired outcomes we all wanted. I shared it with Kevin. A chronic micromanager, he requested multiple changes to the plan. Once the topics were aligned with Kevin's feedback, he begrudgingly agreed to the meeting.

My team jumped into action and made the necessary arrangements to ensure coverage with minimal distractions. We activated our email out-of-office messages, notifying internal customers that we would be out for a short time and provided backup contact information.

The next day, we loaded the van and headed to our destination. My team was beaming with excitement and anticipation. They'd been on trips like this before and understood our retreat's potential. As we drove, we connected on both personal and professional levels. We talked optimistically about how we could advance our vision of being industry leaders and indispensable partners.

When we arrived, we were escorted into our business partner's innovation lab, where all of the futuristic designs inspired us. Next, we moved into a creative thinking lab to begin formulating ideas and developing plans.

Then, the first email hit... And another... And another. A series of 10 or more emails from Kevin appeared on our phones within thirty minutes. He was following up on projects, providing feedback, and checking in to let us know he was there.

His last email's subject line read, "TURN OFF YOUR OUT-OF-OFFICE MESSAGE."

In the body of the email, Kevin wrote that having our out-of-office message turned on sent the wrong message to leadership and internal customers. It was our job to be accessible regardless of what we were doing or who was covering for us.

Ugh. Really? If that isn't micromanagement, I don't know what is.

I looked around the room and saw discouragement, frustration, and anger on the faces of my team members. Some became distracted and anxious. Everyone began to mentally disengage from the creative discussion.

During a break, I gathered my team to ask their thoughts about the emails. They told me they went to great lengths to ensure our time away would be productive and that no initiatives would suffer as a result of our absence. Kevin's micromanagement left them feeling disenfranchised. They wondered if it was a mistake to take the trip.

I asked the team to return to the meeting and told them I'd gently respond to Kevin's emails. I asked them not to make a mountain out of a molehill and turn off the out-of-office messages. Lastly, I encouraged them to stay focused on the purpose of our meeting.

The good news is that the team returned to the meeting and developed a visionary plan. Additionally, I ran interference by responding to Kevin's emails. By engaging Kevin on behalf of the team, I was able to satisfy his need to feel in control. We didn't hear from him again during our trip.

A controlling supervisor can impede your progress and undermine your self-assurance by constantly questioning your decisions and expecting you to be available at all hours. Unsurprisingly, studies indicate that workers' performance declines when they are continually scrutinized.

If your boss is hovering, speak up and ask for the space you need. The reality is that your desire for appropriate autonomy and time is rooted in your drive to produce excellent results. Here are a few practical steps to help you get more breathing room while keeping the relationship intact:

Look at yourself first. Are you meeting expectations? Sometimes micromanaging happens because your boss feels uncertain about your reliability. Once you're sure you're delivering, focus on managing their triggers. Do they stress over deadlines or need constant updates? Plan your next move by getting ahead of those triggers—give updates or clarity *before* they ask.

Clarify Your Role. Pay attention to what your boss values most. Whether it's specific processes or managing schedules, aligning with their preferences makes things smoother and shows you're tuned in. Often, micromanaging is a symptom of unclear or misaligned expectations, which can be easily and enjoyably corrected.

Ask for Feedback. Seek out feedback regularly. Ask specific questions about what they expect and how you can meet those standards. Utilize their input to refine your skills and capitalize on your strengths.

Give Praise for Progress. If your boss gives you more autonomy or supports your ideas, acknowledge it. A little appreciation goes a long way and can encourage them to provide you with more freedom. On some level, your accomplishments do hinge on your management. I know, *shocker!*

If you're working to live out your faith in the workplace, here are some other principles I recommend:

1. *Remember Who You're Working For.* The Bible says, "Work willingly at whatever you do, as though you were working for the Lord rather than for people." (Colossians 3:23 NLT) If you keep your eyes on God and embrace the fact that you're ultimately working for Him, you'll maintain a positive attitude regardless of the circumstances.
2. *Service Is Key.* It's easy to work for a great boss. The hard part is working for and serving a bad one. The Bible says, "You who are servants, be good servants to your masters— *not just to good masters, but also to bad ones. What counts*

is that you put up with it for God's sake when you're maltreated for no good reason." (1 Peter 2:18–19 The Message)
3. *Use wise words.* I disciplined myself to communicate positively and not show irritation if I became frustrated. And I occasionally succeeded! The Bible says, "A gentle answer deflects anger, but harsh words make tempers flare." (Proverbs 15:1 NLT)

Despite desperate circumstances, I grew leaps and bounds during the three years I worked with Kevin—not in spite of him, but in large part because of his style.

You might be wondering why I kicked off with a story about micromanagement and what it means to be a good employee. Here's why: leadership starts with leading yourself. Whether you're a manager or an employee, it's about bringing your best self to work every day. It's not just about what you do when you're faced with a challenging situation—it's how you handle it that really counts. Your mindset, patience, and willingness to focus on solutions will define your growth and positively impact those around you. Lead yourself with grace and resilience, and you'll find a way to thrive, even when the pressures are on.

Managing a micromanager is one thing, but creating a culture where micromanagement doesn't even have room to breathe? That's the real challenge.

CULTURE ISN'T OPTIONAL

Culture isn't just something nice to have. It's the air your team breathes. If they're disengaged, the first step is to look in the mirror and ask, "Am I fully in?" (that's the self-leadership I mentioned above) Building a culture where people show up and engage takes real commitment. I've had the privilege of leading two engagement teams at Coca-Cola, a decade apart, and here's the reality: there's no secret recipe for engagement. The tools are right in front of us—we just need to use them.

Defining Employee Engagement: Stirring Up Discretionary Effort

Employee engagement revolves around the level of *discretionary* effort employees are willing to invest, based on their relationship with their manager and the work environment.

Gallup says 70% of employee engagement boils down to one thing: the manager, your manager.[58] Engagement is really about discretionary effort (i.e., the amount of optional effort you're willing to give), and regardless of our best intentions, the relationship you have with your boss does impact this.

To make the point, I like to ask those in my workshops, "How many of you have had a great boss?" Hands shoot up. Then I follow with, "How many of you have had a bad boss?"—and even more hands go up. That's when I step in with a grin and say, "If you're sitting next to your boss, maybe keep that hand down."

I know what it's like to be fully engaged—charging ahead, giving it everything I've got. You wake up ready to take on the day, excited about the work ahead. But I also know the flip side—those mornings where getting out of bed feels like a struggle, and you're dreading what's coming. There's a world of difference between saying, "Thank God it's morning!" and muttering, "Oh God, it's morning."

Engagement is personal, and I've felt both extremes. So, what's the difference? It often comes down to leadership.

When it comes to employee engagement, the gap between going the extra mile and holding back is obvious.

Discretionary Effort (Going the Extra Mile)	Holding Back (Not Going the Extra Mile)
Sees a problem, steps up, and fixes it—even if it's not their job.	Does just enough to get by and mentally clocks out.
Stays late, comes in early—whatever it takes to get it done.	Avoids extra work like it's the plague.
Jumps in to help a teammate without being asked.	Barely lifts a finger for colleagues.
Raises their hand for new projects and responsibilities.	Hides in the back row when opportunities pop up.
Goes out of their way to make sure the customer leaves happy.	Sticks to the script or policy manual, even if it frustrates the customer.
Offers creative solutions without waiting to be asked.	Keeps their head down and sticks to the status quo.
Learns new skills on their own time to level up.	Stays in their lane and refuses to grow.
Brings energy and positivity that lifts the whole team.	Shows up with a "just here to get paid" attitude.

We've all been there—when you've got a good leader, you give your best. When you don't, you don't. Engagement, or the lack thereof, begins with the manager.

Engagement isn't manipulation. It's about creating the right environment where people want to bring their best. You don't need to push harder; you need to inspire them to give more.

The most significant thing you can do as a leader is build a thriving culture and drive engagement.

I remember someone asking Sandy Douglas, the former president of Coca-Cola North America, how to improve the stock price. His answer was simple: "If we focus on executing the strategy, the stock price will take care of itself." I feel the same way about culture and engagement. When you foster a strong culture, engagement, collaboration, innovation, and productivity naturally follow.

We've all heard the saying, "The end justifies the means," as if the outcome is all that matters. I see it differently: the means justify the end. How you treat your people and how you build the culture—that's where the real advantage lies.

When you focus on *how* you lead, the results will follow. It's not just about hitting the numbers; it's about creating an environment where your team is engaged, trust is built, and success is something you can sustain.

It's simple: if employees have an exceptional boss and a supportive work environment, they will be engaged.

Engaged employees bring their best selves to work every day, actively recommend the company to others, and remain loyal. They thrive in an environment where trust, pride, and positive relationships flourish.

Building a Foundation: The Crucial Role of Company Culture

Let's circle back to company culture—the invisible force that holds everything together. It's more than cool perks and trendy office furniture. Culture is the blend of values, vision, mission, and purpose that drives a successful business. It permeates every part of the company and directly influences how people work and interact within it.

As Gallup says, culture is simply "how we do things around here." It's what sets a team or organization apart and answers the deeper question of why they exist. But here's the kicker—only 41 percent of employees say they really know what their company stands for and what makes it different. Even worse, less than half feel like their company's mission or purpose makes their job matter.[59]

When culture is in sync with purpose and vision, it becomes a powerful driver of engagement and success.

The Business Case for Employee Engagement

When engagement drops, your culture starts to stink. Remember, it's the *discretionary* (read: optional) effort that makes the difference. But when it's thriving, the air is filled with energy and creativity that pulls people in.

I love leading workshops and delivering keynotes on this exact topic—helping organizations see that engagement isn't just "nice-to-have." It's the backbone of success. What drives employee engagement? It begins with providing people with meaningful work that demonstrates how they contribute to fulfilling the company's vision and mission. It's about offering growth opportunities, recognizing their efforts, and leading with integrity.

Employees need to feel a sense of belonging, know precisely what's expected of them, and see how their work fits into the bigger picture.

Quenching the Thirst for Excellence: Our Adventure in Elevating Engagement

My two experiences drive home the importance of employee engagement.

The first was during a tough turnaround. Following a restructuring, the Northeast and Southeast regions were merged, and as expected, their cultures didn't naturally blend well. Engagement scores, measured by Willis Towers Watson (WTW), came in lower than the overall company, internal peers, and even external benchmarks. The region was falling short of its annual targets. That's when the new VP made a pivotal decision—he put employee engagement at the forefront.

In the second scenario, ten years later and with a different team, we set out to take a strong organization from good to great.

With solid leadership in place, a new team was built with a clear vision: create a unique team identity and make the organization a destination for top talent. The WTW engagement scores were already on par with the company, peers, and benchmarks, but the VP wasn't satisfied with just meeting the mark. He aimed to take the organization to the next level and push for excellence.

Here's what we did in both scenarios:

1. We began with the WTW engagement survey, soliciting a high level of participation and encouraging employees to share genuine feedback.
2. Secured a sponsor (e.g., regional vice president) with the authority to make decisions was key. They helped provide the resources and cleared the path for change.
3. We built a team of passionate engagement champions committed to making a difference. To foster connection, we took the team to Universal Studios for some fun and team building before diving into the survey results.
4. We analyzed the data, grouped the key themes, and held candid discussions to understand the root causes of engagement challenges. Each team member was assigned questions to dig deeper into the feedback.
5. We identified areas for improvement, such as trust, communication, and operational effectiveness, and established micro teams to address each issue. Teams conducted interviews, developed action plans, and aligned with leadership on the path forward.
6. Communication was critical. We created a clear plan to keep everyone—from sponsors to team ambassadors—in the loop and engaged throughout the process.
7. The Company administered another WTW survey one year later to measure progress.

Initiatives that Ignited Engagement

We didn't just install a patch into an operating system; we downloaded an entirely different one. Our new meeting formats focused on performance *and* people. We saw the meetings as opportunities to learn more about one another, team building, and have honest conversations with leadership. We began each meeting with some type of recognition related to success stories, learnings, or special contributions.

It also helped to define everyone's roles and responsibilities so that they knew how they fit into the bigger story. We fostered diversity by ensuring that everyone felt valued and had their voice heard.

The Formula for Success: Valuing, Empowering, and Appreciating Employees

I'm proud to say our efforts paid off both times. Our engagement scores not only surpassed those of The Coca-Cola Company but also outperformed internal peer groups and external benchmarks. Even better, we met or exceeded our business goals in the process. It was some of my most meaningful work and significant contributions of my career. The "sweet smell of success" is real, and everyone can sense it.

Here's what we realized: there's no secret formula for employee engagement. It's not just about what you do—it's how you do it that truly matters. By valuing our people and showing real appreciation, we unlocked the full potential of our organization. The how—the way we lead, communicate, and support our teams—makes all the difference in creating an environment where employees thrive.

FIX THE BOY, FIX THE WORLD

I recently shared the story of "The Little Boy Who Put the World Back Together"[60] on a podcast. Here's the quick version: A dad comes home, exhausted after a long day, and his son wants to play. The dad, needing some downtime, grabs a magazine. When the boy keeps asking to play, the dad rips off the cover with a picture of the world on it, tears it into pieces, and gives it to his son, figuring it'll keep him busy. Minutes later, the boy's back, puzzle solved. Surprised, the dad asks how he did it so fast. The boy explains that there was a picture of a little boy on the back, and he knew if he put the boy together, the world would come together too.

This analogy hits the heart of the How>What philosophy. When you get the employee-management relationship right, the results fall into place. That's the essence of leadership and culture-building—focus on the *how*, and the *what* will follow.

When you focus on building strong relationships between employees and management, it's just like the boy putting the world back together. He knew that once he fixed the person, everything else would fall into place.

THE GIRDLER EFFECT: CONFLICT TO CONNECTION

The bottom line is that management and employees need each other to succeed. *How* you get there is just as important—if not more important—than *what* you accomplish. I think my great-great-uncle, Tom Girdler, figured this out later in his career.

Tom was the president of Republic Steel, one of the major players alongside U.S. Steel and Bethlehem Steel. His time at Republic was anything but smooth, marked by intense clashes with labor unions, including the Memorial Day massacre of 1937, when steelworkers in Chicago protested for better conditions and pay. It turned violent, with ten people killed and over one hundred injured, all because Tom refused to back down to the union's demands.[61]

He stepped down as president but stayed on as chairman of the board, eventually becoming CEO of Consolidated-Vultee Aircraft (Convair). His leadership in scaling steel and aircraft production during World War II was critical, and Harvard University later named him one of the "Great American Business Leaders of the 20th Century."[62]

Growing up, Tom's autobiography, *Boot Straps*, was always sitting on the shelf at home, but I didn't crack it open until a few years ago. In it, I found a quote that really struck me. After all the conflicts with labor, he wrote the following.

"The job, as I see it, is to eradicate the false idea that the interest of the employer and the interest of the employees are distinct. In final analysis their interest is the same. Furthermore, it is vitally necessary to improve the liaison mechanism so that the executives of a company know precisely what the men are thinking and feeling; but as an equally vital arrangement, the men must be helped to understand the problems of their company."[63]

That hit home for me. As someone who champions employee engagement, it made perfect sense. Management and employees rely on each other—it's a two-way street. It's not just about *what* you achieve in business; it's about *how* you treat people and engage with them along the way. Tom realized that leaders need to know what their people are thinking and feeling, just like employees need to understand the challenges the company faces.

This approach can be melted down to one word: engagement.

But we've all had enough of fake engagement. I'm challenging you and your team to be honest and genuine with each other. Instead of shying away from conflict, embrace it as a sign that you're on track to actually hear and understand each other.

HOW TO MAKE EMPLOYEE ENGAGEMENT STICK

Ever notice how sticky notes always seem to fall off a flip chart? It turns out that it's usually because the adhesive isn't being used correctly. I picked up a little hack during a design thinking session—if you rotate the sticky note 90 degrees and pull off the adhesive strip vertically, it'll stick much longer. Don't believe me? Give it a try.

What's a sticky note got to do with employee engagement? Just like sticky notes, many organizations attempt to implement engagement initiatives, but they often fail to stick. But what if you approached employee engagement from a different angle? Over the years, leading various engagement initiatives, I've noticed four phases of engagement, and I've learned two ways to make them stick.

The Four Phases of Employee Engagement

As displayed in the chart, I've observed four Employee Engagement phases, including rewiring, results, rumors, and re-org.

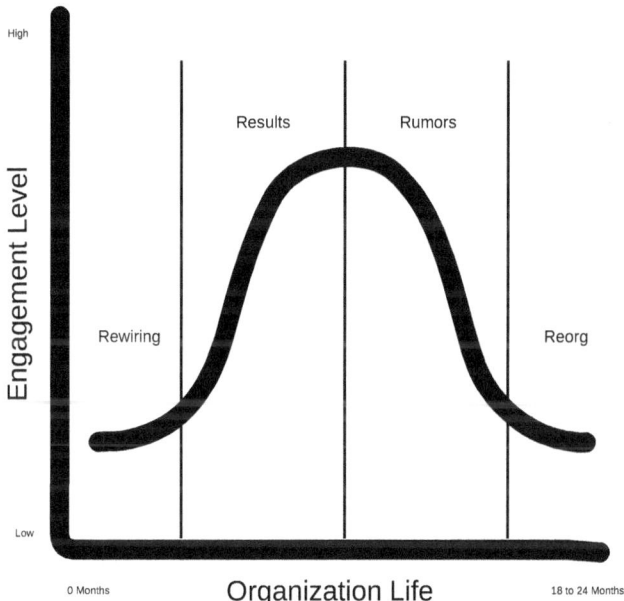

- *Rewiring phase.* The new organization is announced, people are assigned new roles, and the rewiring (i.e., how signals flow through the wires) typically takes six to eight months. Employee engagement lurches higher, but productivity is low.

- *Results phase.* Once the organization understands its vision, mission, and how it works to get things done, results materialize. At some point during the phase, upper management determines there is a need to focus on employee engagement. Committees are formed, charters are written, macro-level strategies are developed, and tactics are deployed. Employee engagement peaks with the proper emphasis, resulting in high productivity.
- *Rumors phase.* Changes in an organization are inevitable, and people begin to speculate. Surely enough, consultants are engaged, and HR representatives huddle in meetings. Employee engagement ebbs, and productivity recedes.
- *Reorg phase.* The phase is filled with posturing, anxiety, and fear, no matter how management rolls out the reorganization communication. People sit on their hands and wait for the news about their jobs. Once their job status is determined, some people exit immediately, while others stay and apply for open roles. It's cold. It's hard. Engagement emphasis stops. It's no wonder that employee engagement is at its lowest point and productivity is minimal during a reorganization.

Then the process starts all over again. Organizations will never reach their potential if stymied by relentless instability.

Moving Toward Sticky Employee Engagement

A senior executive once asked me about my experience with employee engagement and whether engagement can be improved in the long term. I shared my thoughts on the above four phases and clarified that durable engagement improvement depends on two factors.

First, the organization must sustain its "results phase" and continue to progress toward its vision and mission as a team. If the results phase is prolonged, the organization can reach its full potential, whether in terms of financial performance, innovation, or customer satisfaction.

The second part of the solution is to focus on "micro-leadership." The manager-direct report relationship is foundational. If the connection is strong, the organization will flourish. If weak, the organization will flounder.

To create sticky employee engagement regardless of the organizational circumstances, we need to develop leadership skills at the micro level, between managers and direct reports, where the rubber meets the road, including:

- *Expressing empathy.* Understand others, ask questions, listen, put yourself in someone else's shoes, and show them you care.
- *Building trust.* Do what you say you will do, let others know who you are, share your values, and what you stand for.
- *Instilling purpose and meaning.* Help associates understand why their roles exist, how their contribution adds value, and what success looks like.
- *Coaching and developing.* Conduct 360-degree assessments to identify strengths and skill gaps, create capability plans, hold frequent development discussions, and help others reach their potential.
- *Appreciating and encouraging.* Ensure associates know that they are valued and make a difference. Lift them during adversity and lavish praise when they succeed.

Morale is an Organization's Best Friend

Speaking of morale, I recently read an article in The Wall Street Journal about the lessons learned thus far from the Ukraine-Russia war. The author wrote, "The importance of morale to military success isn't a new concept. More than two centuries ago, French emperor, Napoleon said morale was three times as important as the manpower and equipment on the battlefield, in a remark sometimes translated as: "In war, moral power is to physical as three parts out of four." Ukrainian troops, convinced of their moral cause and knowing they were fighting for the survival of their families and their country, beat back Russian forces who were involved in what they were told was a special military operation."[64]

Morale is your organization's best friend.

Here's the reality: it's not just what you do to drive employee engagement—it's how you do it that really counts. Nail the how, and the what—the results—will follow.

LEADING BY LETTING GO

In 2017, a Vice President gathered all his direct reports for a meeting. He had noticed something different in how I led the Coca-Cola Refreshments (CCR) transition during the "System of the Future" initiative. With fourteen market units and only eight employees spread across the country, micromanagement wasn't an option. I had to learn how to delegate, but more importantly, I had to give them the ability to own their work, make decisions, and have a real impact.

Empowerment isn't just about handing off tasks. It's about teaching, guiding, and empowering your people to make decisions and solve problems independently. And it's not just about the wins—empowerment is also about supporting your team when things don't go as planned.

During that meeting, I shared how I led these market units by having my team members take full ownership of their roles. Some markets thrived, others faced challenges, but over time, every person on my team grew because they had the mix of both support and freedom to figure things out.

Empowering your team doesn't just deliver better results—it defines the culture of your organization. When people feel empowered, it's like a fresh breeze hits the workplace.

One of the VP's direct reports said, "Preston, if you do that, they won't need you."

I smiled and replied, "Exactly."

That response took me back to my own experiences of being micromanaged—feeling powerless, disengaged, and frustrated. I learned the hard way that controlling leaders destroy engagement. As I wrapped up my thoughts, it became clear to everyone in the room that empowering our associates wasn't just a leadership style. It was the only way to realize growth and long-term success.

Are you empowering your team to take ownership, or are you holding on to control? Sometimes, the best leadership lessons come from learning what not to do. Teach, guide, and then step back. Let your team take the lead. Your role as a leader is to work yourself out of a job by building a team that doesn't need you to succeed.

REVERSE THE MODEL; REVEAL THE IMPACT

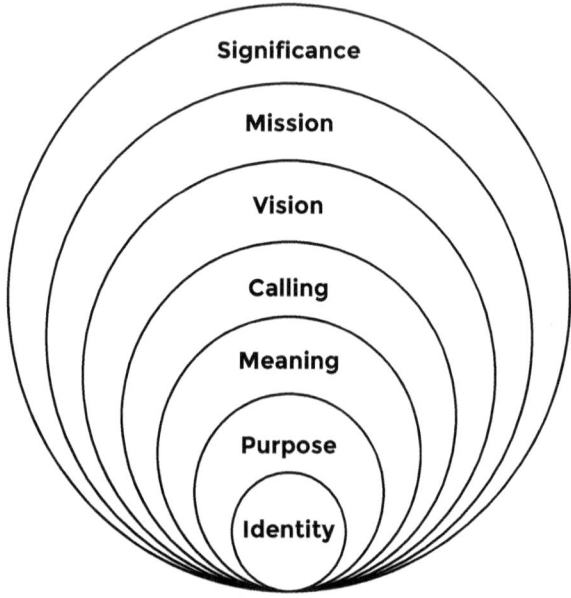

Let's flip the script and start with the end in mind. When we reverse-engineer the How>What model, it forces us to focus on the how we achieve significance, not just what we accomplish. Leadership isn't just about hitting numbers or reaching goals; it's about the journey that gets you there. By working backward from significance, we uncover how mission, vision, calling, meaning, purpose, and identity all work together. This gives us a clear path to building culture and driving engagement because, at the end of the day, it's the *how* that shapes everything else.

Creating a thriving culture and driving engagement are the most significant things you can do as a leader. That's the real impact of leadership—building something that outlasts you. *Significance* is what we're all aiming for—leaving an impact that sticks.

But what powers that significance? It's *mission*. Mission is what pushes us forward. When the mission is clear and tied to something meaningful, everyone knows their role. That's what gives your leadership momentum.

Before that comes *vision*. Vision is about seeing beyond the present, looking ahead to what could be. Vision gives people hope, something to believe in, and a clear direction forward. It's what keeps us pushing through the hard days.

Can you hear that? It's your *calling* - what drew you into leadership in the first place. It's never been about promotion, power, or prestige—it's that deep sense that you are meant to lead and make a positive difference. When things get tough, your calling keeps you grounded and steady.

Next is *meaning*. Meaning shows up in the everyday actions that align with your purpose. When people can see how their daily work connects to something bigger, they find meaning. That's what turns the mundane into something worthwhile.

Then there's purpose. Purpose is the fuel that drives everything. It's what answers the question of "why" you do what you do. Purpose is what gets you moving in the morning, even when the going gets tough. It's what keeps your focus on creating real impact, not just hitting the numbers.

At the core of everything is *identity*—who you are as a leader and what you stand for. Without identity, none of the other layers hold. It's your identity that shapes your leadership and sets the foundation for the culture you build.

Reverse-engineering the *How>What* model makes one thing clear: significance doesn't just happen by chance. It's built on a strong foundation of identity, purpose, meaning, and a mission driven by a clear vision. When you work backward, you uncover the *how* behind real leadership—how you build trust, spark engagement, and help others reach their potential.

Focus on the *how* and watch the results fall into place.

THE SMELL OF SUCCESS: IT'S IN THE HOW

The reality is, success isn't about what we achieve—it's about how we get there.

It's how we engage with people and how we create environments where they feel respected, valued, and appreciated. That's the scent of a thriving culture. Just like the smell of a Napa vineyard or the stench left behind by a garbage truck, leadership leaves a lasting scent. When we focus on the how, the what—lasting impact and meaningful results—naturally follow. It's the shift from focusing solely on outcomes to investing in the process that unlocks the full potential of our teams and organizations. Leadership leaves a lasting scent—one that everyone picks up on. When you focus on the how, you build a culture that not only smells like success but also keeps it going strong.

PRINCIPLE
Culture = How

QUESTIONS

What's the "scent" of your culture, and how does it reflect how you lead? What can you do to ensure your leadership is shaping a culture that thrives?

_____
_____
_____

Are you more focused on *what* your team delivers or *how* engaged they are with their team and their work? How can you shift your focus to make sure you're driving real connection and investment from your people, and not just results?

_____
_____
_____

How are you empowering your team to take ownership of their work and collaborations? Are you giving them the trust and space to make decisions, or are you holding on too tightly? What can you do to help them feel confident, trusted, and capable of driving success?

_____
_____
_____

EPILOGUE

True Identity

> "I know *what* I want to say,
> but I'm not sure *how* to say it."
> —ME, IN EVERY CHAPTER OF THIS BOOK

I began writing a book that would be true to who I am —a Christian —while expressing my biblical worldview covertly. (More on this in a moment.) I was trying to figure out how to gesture to God without mentioning him, let alone including him, in what I want to share with you. I found the attempt exhausting and futile.

Here I was writing about identity and authenticity, yet I wasn't being true to who I am. I'd rather be integrous and sell fewer books, rather than merely articulate human theories to broaden my reach. So, if you're reading this and you aren't what I call "faith forward," a few things to consider.

First, I've one clear goal: to pour my soul into words that will make a positive difference in your life and career, as I've seen these principles help so many others.

Second, I have a biblical worldview, as opposed to a natural, transcendental, or postmodern one. That means I believe that God created us in His image, sin disfigures and disrupts His image in us, Christ died for our sins to redeem us and make us new, and we can actively participate with God to restore things to the way they were meant to be—a healthy state.

Third, I also know that we all have a conscience, a general sense of right and wrong, of what is good and what is bad—a moral compass. I believe that one only needs to look at wrong or evil in the world – dictatorships, human trafficking, slavery, violent crime, racism, toxic workplaces, and more—to see that something is horribly wrong and broken in the world. We have a great propensity to do good or bad, but we are more inclined toward the negative or selfish because of sin.

If there is evil, there must also be good. And the good is what I want to appeal to. Why? Because I believe we can experience "shalom" in our workplaces, communities, and schools.

Here's what I mean. "Shalom is a universal flourishing, wholeness, and delight – a rich state of affairs in which natural needs are satisfied and natural gifts fruitfully employed, a state of affairs that inspires joyful wonder as the creator and savior opens doors and speaks welcome to the creatures in whom he delights. Shalom, in other words, is the way things are supposed to be."[65]

That's where our conscience comes in. I believe in what Abraham Lincoln called the "better angels of our nature"—the positive impulses of good. Even though we're created in God's image, sin has twisted that original goodness. Our nature may lean toward selfishness, but by God's grace, we can still reflect His goodness when inspired.

Whether or not you're a faith-forward individual, we can all work together when there's a common vision, shared values, and a mission to make things better.

What if I said to you that results matter? You'd probably nod your head in agreement. Results are table stakes; they keep you in the game, keep you employed, prolong your career. But often the means don't justify the end. Have you ever experienced a toxic work environment or a tyrannical boss? Maybe the results were there, but the environment was hell. I've been there.

How you do something matters, even more so than what you do. That's leadership.

Embracing this philosophy transformed my life and revealed principles that extend far beyond my own experience.

THE JOURNEY OF TRANSFORMATION

My journey as a follower of Jesus began in 1980. As a young teenager, I responded to the call of faith and accepted the Lord into my life. This decision set the foundation for everything that followed. Yet, it wasn't until 2005, in the midst of a challenging career at The Coca-Cola Company, that I truly surrendered my professional life to Him.

The How>What philosophy that I've shared throughout this book is not just a leadership principle; it reflects my personal transformation. For years, I excelled in the "what" of my career – achieving goals, hitting targets, and climbing the corporate ladder. However, it was the "how" that required a deeper look at myself.

In 2005, I faced a pivotal moment. Two associates quit my team in quick succession, leaving me to question my approach and leadership. It was a humbling experience, one that drove me to my knees in surrender. I realized that while I was proficient in delivering results, I had neglected the importance of how I treated those around me. My identity had been rooted in my *performance*—and the performance of those around me—rather than who I was in Christ.

Surrendering my career to Jesus marked the beginning of a transformative process, during which I learned to lead with integrity, compassion, and a servant's heart. This shift not only changed my professional trajectory but also deepened my faith and commitment to living out my beliefs in every aspect of my life.

The first chapter of this book, "Start with Who?" underscores the importance of finding our identity. But one's identity can only be found in the One who created us. It is from this foundation that all other aspects of our lives flow. When we understand who we are in Christ, it transforms how we approach our work, relationships, and challenges. The How>What philosophy is about prioritizing character and integrity over mere achievements, understanding that our actions reflect our deeper beliefs and values.

TIME TO FLY: REFLECTIONS ON MY LAST DAY AT THE COCA-COLA COMPANY

I was writing this on a plane to somewhere, thinking about retiring from The Coca-Cola Company after 21.5 years. That's almost 8,000 days, or 192,000 hours —nearly 40% of my life — working for one employer. I resolved to stay with Coke after job-hopping across different companies (e.g., AmSouth Bank, Ralston Purina, Dale Carnegie Training, and Hershey Chocolate).

A friend told me that once folks become part of the beverage industry, they typically stay. But staying long-term was always uncertain. Like I've said, I've often compared working at TCCC to being a member of Congress. You're up for re-election every two years, and once elected, your campaign starts all over again. I've experienced eleven reorganizations, averaging about one every two years. I've been mapped into roles, involuntarily relocated, and displaced. Some positions were an absolute joy, and others not so much. Often, the work experience came down to the relationship with my manager. I've worked with and for some terrific leaders. I've also worked for some tyrants. Perhaps, like you, I modeled what I saw in the great ones and learned from the deficiencies of the others. Leadership is better caught than taught.

I finally learned that my career did not define who I am. Honestly, my veins didn't run Coke red. My priorities were different than most. I put my faith and family above my career.

I always wanted to perform well and deliver results. For about half of my time at TCCC, I was focused on myself, my reputation, and my ambitions. It wasn't until midstream that God got hold of me, and I began to understand that people matter more than performance. I realized that focusing on people, helping them become the best version of themselves, and creating a positive work environment meant more than a maniacal focus on results. Said another way, the *how* trumps the *what*. Putting others first typically led to solid results. (Much of my transformation is captured in my book, *Discipled Leader*.)

I never ascended to the once-desired role of vice president. Sometimes, I look back and wonder why. But at the end of that chapter of my career, I have more of a big-picture view: *position doesn't equal influence*.

After all, if my ultimate goal in life is significance (and it is), God only knows where I can have the most impact. The higher you go in an organization doesn't necessarily equate to the level of impact you achieve. I didn't need to be a VP or lead an organization to be influential.

I walked away from the company thankful for my tenure, looking to the future, moving out in faith, not knowing where I was going but trusting God—following the call to help people become the best version of themselves and become redemptive workplace influencers. Or, in Coke speak, refreshing the world and making a positive difference.

My retirement party was a special night. My last one as a Coca-Cola associate in the Atlanta Office Complex (AOC, as it's affectionately called). Surrounded by family, friends, and longtime colleagues. Everyone shared a small anecdote or takeaway about our relationship. In turn, I shared something back to affirm them.

Lord, we did it right, in the long run, I prayed. *They saw my faith in you, my family-first mindset, and desire to make the workplace better. Thank you for allowing me to love others well, to make a positive difference, and to grow in you.*

FINDING IDENTITY IN THE GARDEN

A few months after retiring from Coke, Carla and I, along with some friends, went on a Passion City Church Holy Land Tour. There I was, sitting in the Garden of Gethsemane. Maybe you've heard of it, a little garden where Jesus submitted his life to God before he went to the Cross. A weighty place to say the least.

I'd recently taken early retirement, and after being untethered from Coke, I was drifting—the structure, the accolades, the challenge, the sense of importance that came from my corporate life all vanished. I was grappling with a loss of identity, a crisis of purpose.

"Lord, where are you in all of this," I implored.

In the garden, where Jesus himself grappled with his destiny, I found a semblance of solace.

He whispered, "Follow me," two words I'll never forget hearing.

It was a directive that required no roadmap, no strategic plan, no business acumen. It was a call to surrender, to trust, to let go of the what and why, and to embrace the *who*.

Os Guinness speaks of calling as a summons by God that infuses our very existence with meaning. And in that moment, I realized that my identity wasn't tied to my past achievements or future endeavors—it was anchored in Jesus. It was about being His, first and foremost.

The world tells us to find our purpose through self-exploration and experiences, but I've come to understand that it's not about crafting our narrative—it's about stepping into the one already written for us. It's about responding to the call of Jesus, the most revolutionary invitation ever extended.

Have you heard his call, "Follow Me"? If you've heard it and haven't responded, what's holding you back? Answering his call will be one of the most significant decisions you've ever made.

With my identity firmly anchored in Jesus, I began to see how a personal transformation could extend beyond myself to impact the world around me.

Reflecting on my journey, it hit me that the path I'd walked wasn't always upward, or even forward. Whose is, right? It was more like a ripple effect, a series of circles, each one bringing me back to the existential questions of identity, purpose, and meaning. Every twist and turn deepened my understanding of what it means to follow Jesus.

In that moment, I saw it clearly: concentric circles, moving from that initial call, "Follow Me," to living a life of significance. It wasn't just a leadership framework; it was God's way of shaping me, and it continues to guide me.

Here's how the model looks based on Jesus's call to follow him:

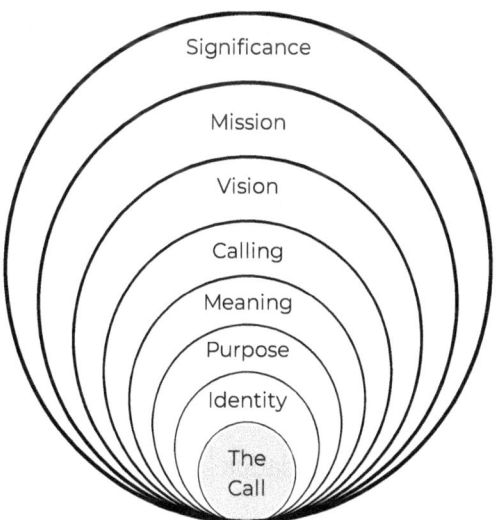

The Call. "Follow me." The starting point with Jesus is a pivotal moment. It is the foundation for our journey and a continuing opportunity to a greater purpose—being part of His story.

Identity. When you follow Jesus, you become more and more secure in the truth that you're a child of God. This stage of the journey provides a sense of belonging and worth that's based on God's grace and not our accomplishments. It's about whose you are—that's what shapes who you are.

Purpose. Emanating from our identity, we discover our purpose: to glorify God by enjoying Him forever. Building on this, my purpose statement is to glorify God, advance his kingdom, and equip people.

Meaning. As we start to see the impact of our purpose, meaning emerges. We gain a sense of fulfillment and understanding that our efforts make a difference.

Calling. We often associate this with our careers. But in light of following Jesus, calling represents a deeper understanding of how to live out our purpose in a practical, everyday sense, in the workplace and beyond.

Vision & Mission. These guideposts provide more specific direction. Vision is a picture of who you want to be when you grow up, a sense of what the future looks like, while mission defines the steps to get there.

Significance. At the highest level, a significant life means living beyond ourselves—impacting others, leaving a legacy, and finding joy in serving God and others for the greater good. Remarkably, God's Word reveals that our significance can extend even into eternity.

The layering reveals a natural progression that begins inward and then expands outward, shaping the world around us. Form before function, being before doing. Starting from the right place—Jesus' call—sets the sure foundation for a fulfilling and impactful life.

I'm humbled and amazed that I have the honor of coaching leaders, consulting with businesses and nonprofits, and speaking at events. Who knows? Maybe I'll positively influence more people in this season of life than I did at Coke.

EMBRACE YOUR TRANSFORMATIVE JOURNEY

As you finish this book, I encourage you to reflect on how you approach your daily tasks and interactions. Remember that true success is not measured by what you accomplish, but by how you inspire and lift those around you.

Thank you for joining me on this journey. My hope and prayer are that you find your identity in Christ and let that guide all you do. May you experience the profound joy and fulfillment that comes from living a life rooted in faith. May you focus on the moments before you and pause to consider not only what you're doing, but also how.

If this book has stirred any questions in you, please feel free to reach out to me. If any of the principles have helped you lead more effectively, I'd also love to hear your story.

PrestonPoore.com

How > What Principles

1. Know your core
2. Drive with purpose
3. Act with vision
4. Connect beyond words
5. Be integrous and trust will follow
6. Build influence, brick by brick
7. Own your fears; never let them own you
8. Develop with intention-both in yourself and others
9. It's not about doing more; it's about doing the right more
10. Strategize boldly, execute relentlessly, improve continuously
11. Don't just manage change, lead it
12. Culture = How

Acknowledgements

Mike Loomis—my sherpa. Thanks for guiding me up the mountain and bringing out the best in me along the way.

Scott Spiewak & Heidi Jensen—grateful for your work to help get this message out into the world. Thanks for joining the journey and championing the vision.

Kevin Marks and Leighton Ching - your advice, belief, and support were game changers.

Chris Darley, Michael Chetelat, Bryan Miller, Kyle Crabtree, Joe Colavito, and Holly Mattingly Cunningham—my Personal Advisory Board. Thanks for believing in me, pushing me, and offering wise counsel every step of the way.

Mom and Dad—shaping my character from the get-go, modeling commitment and generosity, and supporting me during the highs and lows.

My brother, Jeff —not often does one go through life with a close brother, best friend, and business partner like you. I'm blessed, and proud of you.

And to Carla—my wife, my best friend, and my wisest counselor. You've lived every word of this with me. You've challenged me, supported me, and helped me become the man and leader God's called me to be. This book wouldn't exist without you.

I'd also love to acknowledge an organization called CLC (Christ Led Communities). We don't need more Bible studies. We need more transformed men.

That's why CLC changed everything for me. It didn't just deepen my knowledge of God—it deepened my walk with Him. It strengthened my character, sharpened my calling, and surrounded me with men I now call brothers.

CLC equips men to follow Christ, live with purpose, and lead with impact. If you're looking for more than just a weekly study—if you want a life-shaping experience that helps you flourish in faith, family, and leadership—go to www.clchq.org. You won't regret it.

HOW IS GRE>TER THAN WHAT

Master the Growth and Leadership Skill Everyone Else Ignores

PRESTON POORE

WORKBOOK COMPANION

The Free Workbook
That Turns Insight into Action

Reading about growth is one thing. Living it? That's the game-changer.

This free workbook helps you do just that. It's not fluff.

It's a leadership mirror. A growth accelerator. A practical guide to becoming the kind of leader people *want* to follow—not just have to

https://mailchi.mp/prestonpoore/hwworkbook

Formed to Lead

Faith and leadership aren't separate journeys—they're deeply connected. In Discipled Leader, Preston Poore combines decades of Fortune 500 leadership experience with a biblical foundation to deliver:

- A roadmap for integrating your faith into everyday leadership.
- 10 leadership competencies to help you grow influence and effectiveness.
- How to move from being stuck or overwhelmed to leading with clarity, confidence, and purpose.

Available on Amazon or PrestonPoore.com, along with free bonus resources.

21 DAYS TO SOUND DECISION MAKING

How to Grow Your Credibility and Influence
Through Making Better Decisions

PRESTON POORE

Make Better Decisions One Day at a Time

Get your free copy of *21 Days to Sound Decision Making*
A faith-forward guide to thinking clearly, acting wisely, and choosing well.

Because better choices lead to a better life.
https://mailchi.mp/prestonpoore/21days

Transform Your Team.
Learn the *How*.

Leading people is messy. It's full of wins, wipeouts, and "Did I really just say that?" moments.

Preston Poore experienced all off this, and brings those lessons (the good, the bad, and the hilarious) to every talk and workshop.

- Leadership Development
- Communication Excellence
- Personal and Professional Growth
- Influence Without Authority
- Faith in the Workplace
- Problem-Solving and Innovation

He's consulted and trained countless leaders on three continents. Invite Preston to your event and learn the how of leadership.

Coaching and Consulting

It's all about *how* you lead, not just what you accomplish.

I can walk alongside you and your team, and save you time, money, and unnecessary headaches.

We both know this: the how of leadership is the hardest part.

If you want to accelerate your personal growth as a leader—and improve the culture of your organization, let's talk.

PrestonPoore.com

Notes and References

Introduction: How Sunset Cinema Shaped a Leadership Philosophy
1 https://www.history.com/news/costa-concordia-cruise-ship-disaster-sinking-captain
2 https://www.history.com/this-day-in-history/sully-sullenberger-performs-miracle-on-the-hudson

Chapter 1: Start with Who?
3 https://www.thewoodeneffect.com/about-coach/
4 https://www.wsj.com/articles/SB889022953673487500
5 https://www.markwhitacre.com/PDF%20-%20TwoTen%20Magazine%20Issue11%20Mark%20Whitacre.pdf
6 www.psychologytoday.com/us/basics/identity

Chapter 2: Driving with Purpose
7 David Kinnaman and Gabe Lyons, Good Faith: Being Christian When Society Thinks You're Irrelevant and Extreme (Ada, MI: Baker, 2016)
8 https://mcc.gse.harvard.edu/reports/on-edge
9 https://mcc.gse.harvard.edu/whats-new/gen-z-meaning-purpose
10 https://www.nimh.nih.gov/health/statistics/major-depression
11 KFF, "A Look at the Latest Suicide Data and Change Over the Last Decade," Heather Saunders and Nirmita Panchal, Published August 04, 2023.
12 "Suicides in the U.S. reached all-time high in 2022, CDC data shows." August 10, 2023, 5:11 PM EDT / Source: The Associated Press.
13 https://rallyfoundation.org/research/
14 Pew Research Center. "What Makes Life Meaningful? Views From 17 Advanced Economies." Pew Research Center, November 18, 2021. https://www.pewresearch.org/global/2021/11/18/what-makes-life-meaningful-views-from-17-advanced-economies/.
15 "Career Strategy: Don't sell sugar water", CNBC, https://www.cnbc.com/2017/03/24/career-strategy-dont-sell-sugar-water.html
16 https://investors.coca-colacompany.com/about/our-purpose#:~:text=To%20refresh%20the%20world%20and,these%20last%20two%20historic%20years.
17 https://blog.ultatel.com/telephone-facts
18 https://www.invoca.com/blog/20-useful-facts-about-phone-calls-most-marketers-still-dont-know
19 https://modularhomesource.com/45-interesting-facts-about-phone-calls-emails-and-texts/

Chapter 3: The Mission of Vision
20 https://numerica.us/how-numerica-grew-from-humble-beginnings/ and https://natsci.source.colostate.edu/csu-startup-company-numerica-ensures-homeland-security-in-air-missile-and-space-industries/

21 https://willitmaketheboatgofaster.com/speakers/ben-hunt-davis/

Chapter 4: Talk Is Cheap

22 https://lunio.ai/blog/strategy/how-many-ads-do-we-see-a-day/
23 https://wordsrated.com/how-many-words-does-the-average-person-say-a-day/
24 https://www.creditdonkey.com/listening-statistics.html
25 IBID
26 https://socialmediavictims.org/effects-of-social-media/teens-social-skills/
27 https://www.wsj.com/lifestyle/workplace/american-workers-loneliness-research-35793dc4

Chapter 5: Stop Building Trust

28 https://www.justice.gov/opa/pr/two-former-presidents-boilermakers-international-union-among-seven-indicted-20m-embezzlement
29 https://www.usnews.com/news/us/articles/2024-08-23/former-alabama-prosecutor-found-guilty-of-abusing-position-for-sex
30 https://www.independent.co.uk/news/ap-beijing-china-communist-party-xi-jinping-b2518602.html
31 https://www.npr.org/2005/05/11/4647602/in-praise-of-roddick-and-old-fashioned-sportsmanship
32 Kouzes, James M. and Posner, Barry Z. The Leadership Challenge, Hoboken, NJ: John Wiley & Sons, Inc., 2017, pp. 76-78, digital copy

Chapter 6: Titles Don't Matter

33 https://www.johnmaxwell.com/blog/leading-a-life-of-intentional-influence/
34 https://www.vocabulary.com/dictionary/influence
35 Development Dimensions International (DDI), Global Leadership Forecast 2023, p 19
36 IBID, p. 19
37 *Mike Price was hired to replace Dennis Franchione for the 2003 season. He was quickly dismissed after a well-documented off-the-field incident. My only memory of Coach Price was when we held a Coca-Cola Fall Football sales rally in the Bryant-Denny Stadium locker room. Price was our guest speaker, and our intent for him was to inspire our local sales team. When it was time for him to address the crowd, he pulled out a Pepsi-Cola 20 oz bottle, threw it against the lockers, and yelled, "F**K Pepsi." We were in shock. Not the way to start a talk. Extremely unprofessional. I shook my head in disbelief and wondered what we were getting into. Needless to say, Coach Price didn't last very long.*
38 *Working with the University of Alabama was a personal passion of mine. When I was young, I used to watch Alabama football games with my dad. He always pointed out Bear Bryant on the sidelines and talked favorably about him. And most of my extended relatives lived in Alabama. When I moved to Alabama in 1989, I was told I had to choose between Alabama and Auburn (IYKYK). I picked Alabama. But most importantly, my bride attended the University of Alabama. We were season ticket holders and attended the 1992 National Championship game in New Orleans versus the University of Miami. I guess you could say I married "it" (i.e., a passion for all things UA). All of this before working with Coke and leading the University of Alabama relationship for a few years. It was an honor.*

Chapter 7: Dancing with Wolves
39 http://www.jenniferhawthorne.com/articles/change_your_thoughts.html
40 Ibid
41 Maxwell, John C. *The 15 Invaluable Laws of Growth: Live Them and Reach Your Potential.* New York: Center Street, 2012.
42 https://www.verywellmind.com/what-is-displacement-in-psychology-4587375
43 https://www.stopbullying.gov/resources/facts

Chapter 8: Do You Believe?
44 Excerpt From John C. Maxwell & Jim Dornan. "Becoming a Person of Influence." Apple Books. https://books.apple.com/us/book/becoming-a-person-of-influence/id607555354

Chapter 9: The Faithful
45 https://www.mckinsey.com/capabilities/people-and-organizational-performance/our-insights/three-keys-to-faster-better-decisions#
46 https://joinhomebase.com/blog/time-management-statistics/
47 Swindoll, Charles R. Swindoll's Ultimate Book of Illustrations and Quotes. Nashville, TN: Thomas Nelson, 1998

Chapter 10: Plans Don't Win
48 Development Dimensions International. *Global Leadership Forecast 2023*, 19. DDI, 2023. https://www.ddiworld.com/global-leadership-forecast-2023.
49 https://www.historyoasis.com/post/history-of-vanilla-coke
50 https://www.latimes.com/archives/la-xpm-2006-feb-15-fi-buffett15-story.html
51 Tolstoy, Leo. Pamphlets: Translated from the Russian. "Three Methods of Reform," 1900. As cited in Books on the Wall, accessed October 6, 2024. https://booksonthewall.com/blog/leo-tolstoy-quote/.
52 Colson, C. How Now Shall We Live?. Carol Stream, IL: Tyndale, 1999
53 https://www.youtube.com/watch?v=OJqtnawj7fA
54 https://www.bevindustry.com/articles/91736-2019-beverage-bottler-of-the-year-coca-cola-completes-bottling-initiative
55 https://www.walkme.com/blog/change-management-statistics/#:~:text=Key%20Takeaways,-47%25%20of%20organizations&text=Only%2034%25%20of%20change%20initiatives,which%20further%20causes%20transformation%20failure.
56 https://getlucidity.com/strategy-resources/bridges-transition-model/
57 Maxwell, John C., Sometimes You Win, Sometimes You Learn, Center Street, Hachette Book Group USA, Day One 2013, p. 93.

Chapter 11: Change or Be Changed

Chapter 12: What's That Smell?
58 https://www.gallup.com/workplace/285674/improve-employee-engagement-workplace.aspx
59 Gallup, Inc., "Gallup's Approach to Culture: Building a Culture that Drives Performance", 2018, pp.5-7
60 https://cameronfreeman.com/personal/confessions-cult-leader-lifestream-seminar-experience/boy-put-world-story-jim-quinn-founder-lifestream-basic-seminar/

61 https://www.chicagohistory.org/remembering-the-memorial-day-massacre/
62 https://case.edu/ech/articles/g/girdler-tom-mercer
63 Girdler, Tom M., and Boyden Sparkes. *Boot Straps: The Autobiography of Tom M. Girdler*. New York: Charles Scribner's Sons, 1943, p 447
64 https://www.wsj.com/articles/the-conflict-in-ukraine-offers-oldand-newlessons-in-21st-century-warfare-d302e8ea

Epilogue: True Identity

65 Sin: Not the Way It's Supposed to Be, Conelius Plantinga Jr., 2010, Christ Campus Initiative (CCI)

www.ingramcontent.com/pod-product-compliance
Lightning Source LLC
Chambersburg PA
CBHW050856160426
43194CB00011B/2171